HEAVEN
ON EARTH

Also by Danny Seo
Generation React: Activism for Beginners

HEAVEN ON EARTH

15-MINUTE MIRACLES TO CHANGE THE WORLD

DANNY SEO

POCKET BOOKS

NEW YORK   LONDON   TORONTO   SYDNEY   TOKYO   SINGAPORE

POCKET BOOKS, a division of Simon & Schuster Inc.
1230 Avenue of the Americas, New York, NY 10020

ISBN: 0-671-03644-0

First Pocket Books hardcover printing May 1999

10   9   8   7   6   5   4   3   2   1

POCKET and colophon are registered trademarks of
Simon & Schuster Inc.

Designed by Celia Fuller and Laura Lindgren

Printed in the U.S.A. on recycled paper

BP/✕

*For my parents on the occasion
of their thirtieth wedding anniversary*

CONTENTS

Contents

ACKNOWLEDGMENTS

It's been such an honor to work and collaborate with so many hardworking, creative, and talented people.

I am profoundly grateful to Joe Regal, my literary agent, who transforms my dreams into reality. I thank you for believing in me from the start, when no one else thought a teenage "kid" could write books.

I'd like to express a special thanks to Nancy Miller, my editor at Pocket Books, who understood from the start my intentions for writing *Heaven on Earth*. I would also like to thank everyone at Pocket Books for working so hard to bring this book to life.

Also, thank you to A. T. Birmingham-Young at the Giraffe Project for helping me locate all the wonderful miracle workers profiled in this book.

Finally, I'd like to thank my friends, family, and business associates for supporting me throughout my career and for joining me on my quest to create Heaven on Earth.

PREFACE

I'm not going to college." With those five words, I dropped a bombshell on my parents.

I was eighteen years old at the time and performing miserably in high school. I ranked 169th out of 170 students at Governor Mifflin High School in Berks County, Pennsylvania (I moved up from last place after one student dropped out of school). My grade point average was an embarrassing D−; F's dotted my report card in English, civics, and chemistry. (After the ninth grade, my report card started to "mysteriously" disappear in the mail.) As the youngest of three children (both my sister and brother attended Ivy League schools and created a Seo academic myth that took very little time for me to shatter), my parents shook their heads in disbelief at my announcement.

Even though my mother didn't say a word, I knew what she was thinking. Korean-American parents are very competitive, especially in a tightly knit community like Berks County, where every Korean family knows each other very well. Every child is expected to excel in music (dinner parties are often transformed into piano competitions) and academics, and to win awards for being the "Young Leader in 'fill in the blank' of the Year." What was my mother going to tell her friends? How would she face them? Would her youngest son live at home forever? But instead of confronting me with these concerns, she asked if I had any laundry that needed ironing.

My father ended the awkward moment with a question. "Well, what are you going to do?" In perhaps my only act of conforming to the stereotypes of my generation, I stared back at him and uttered, "I dunno."

Just weeks before, I had stepped down as the CEO of Earth 2000 National, a 25,000-member teen organization I founded at age twelve with just $10. From bouncing between offices in Pennsylvania and Chicago to fund-raising on behalf of the organization and giving media interviews, I led an extraordinary life for a teenager. But deep down inside, I knew this aspect of my life was finished. I had accomplished what I originally set out to do, launching campaigns to protect the environment and save endangered animals and inspiring other young people to get involved. I had won dozens of awards, two for lifetime achievement. But the truth was hanging over my head like a thick layer of Los Angeles smog. It was time to move on and pursue my mission.

Ever since I was a young child, I've always believed I had a very specific mission in life. That mission was to show others that they can do extraordinary things if they allow themselves to reach their fullest potential. "Get the maximum amount of work done with the minimum amount of effort!" I often preached to my board members. A few weeks after I stunned my parents with my decision not to attend college, I bewildered them even more: I decided to pursue this mission.

My parents looked at me as if I had just announced I had joined a religious cult. Or, more accurately, as if I had planned to start my own religious cult. Although they expressed much hesitation and doubt about my decision, they supported me nonetheless.

How to pursue my mission was another challenge. With no plan of action or direction, I continued to volunteer regularly with numerous charities and lecture at colleges, and I even wrote a book based on my experiences as the teenage CEO of Earth 2000. But even with these activities, as important as they were, I felt I lacked direction. Of all the influences I could have imagined, I never would have guessed the one that really made a difference: The person who helped me on my path was Oprah Winfrey.

On January 22, 1998, I appeared on *Oprah* to discuss how I raised $30,000 in less than thirty days to pay for the construction of a Habitat for Humanity home. The project was part of her Oprah's Angel Network, the charitable campaign for her popular television talk show. At first, I viewed it as a typical fund-raising project and as an opportunity to shake hands with the most powerful person in entertainment. But to my delight, my encounter with Oprah turned out to be one of the most meaningful five minutes of my entire life.

Producers from the show were familiar with my ability to raise hundreds of thousands of dollars for charities and invited me to raise $30,000 to sponsor one of 205 Habitat for Humanity homes the *Oprah* show was building. Even though I had built up contacts with an impressive network of philanthropists and major corporate CEOs, I was forbidden to ask them for help. I had to use, as requested by the producers, fund-raising skills any viewer could replicate in his or her community. While this involved more work than I really needed to do, I understood their motivations.

After all, while it's wonderful to see major corporations sponsor homes with the quick draft of a check, *Oprah* viewers are not major corporations. Her viewers are people with bills to pay, work to do, and kids who need to be chauffeured to soccer practice, ballet, and club meetings. With a hectic life like that, how could a typical viewer possibly raise $30,000, $10,000, or even $500 to support a worthy project like the Angel Network?

My intention never was to write a book, but only to use my spare time to raise money for Habitat for Humanity. I firmly believed in the good work Ms. Winfrey was doing with her Angel Network, and I just wanted to be part of it; I wanted to show her viewing audience that individuals with enough passion and good common sense could go beyond altruism and change their community—easily.

But after receiving a few hundred E-mails and a steady stream of regular mail from *Oprah* viewers and having people stop me at airports, at the gym, and on the street, saying how inspired they were by my hard work and how I was an "exceptional" human being, I realized I hadn't successfully made the point I wanted to during my five-minute segment. I had honestly believed that once people saw how easy it was to do something "extraordinary," like raising $30,000 in less than thirty days, they would realize it was within their power, too. I thought they would then begin to raise funds themselves. Instead, I saw that I had merely "inspired" them.

The reason hordes of people weren't running out into their communities to raise money and make a difference is that they allowed themselves to accept only the first of the three tenets needed to create Heaven on Earth.

First, you must allow yourself to be inspired and motivated by the work of others. I must admit that when I received the Albert Schweitzer Institute Award in 1995, I knew nothing of the great humanitarian for whom the award was named. But the more I researched his work, from his commitment to protecting the Earth's environment to his efforts to help the sick and neglected in almost every corner of the world, I was inspired. His words have had a great impact on my life: "Example is not the main thing in influencing others. It is the only thing." Words to live by. When you are inspired by another individual, the desire to make a difference becomes part of your soul. Inspiration opens your eyes to the world around you, to all the work that still needs to be done, and the role you will play in changing the world.

Second, you must absorb information like a sponge and use it. If one day, for example, you are inspired to build a table, but have never worked in carpentry before (let alone picked up a hammer), no amount of motivation will get that table built; you need a blueprint and some basic training. The same goes for changing the world. Creating Heaven on Earth can only occur if you educate yourself. But relax. There are no pop quizzes or time-consuming classes to attend; you can take the responsibility to seek out sources of information when you need it. This book, you'll discover, offers a wealth of knowl-edge to get you started. But you can find resources anywhere, even masked as something else. For example, I've used the trendy magazine *Wallpaper* for graphic design ideas when designing a charity's program guide for an annual fund-raiser. Information is everywhere.

Finally, and most important, you must take action. I can't begin to tell you how many times I've attended conferences on "leadership" and seen speakers motivating the audience, workshops educating the audience, and the audience leaving doing nothing. Granted, conference luncheons can be nice, but what's the point? It's action that gets the job done.

I realize that taking action is the most difficult of the three tenets, and that's why Angel Power Rule #1, "Create Miracles: Cliffs Notes–Style," will come in mighty handy. At the end of each chapter, you'll find ten concrete mini-miracles you can perform to help your community or the life of someone in need. And here's my favorite part: *All of them can be done in less than fifteen minutes a day.* Who doesn't have at least fifteen minutes a day to make a difference? These fifteen-minute miracles have become my favorite moments in the day and I hope they will be yours, too.

Once you accept these three tenets, the Ten Rules of Angel Power will be an invaluable primer to help you on your way to Heaven on Earth. These ten rules are the foundation of *Heaven on Earth;* I live my personal, professional, and charitable lives by them. The Ten Rules of Angel Power have allowed me to reach my fullest potential and will serve you well once you adopt them, too.

I've included throughout some personal stories about my work and what motivated me to get started, how I continue to be inspired, and where I find the basic resources to keep going. I hope these stories and the stories of other "ordinary" people doing extraordinary things will show you without a doubt that the Angel Power Rules work.

Creating Heaven on Earth is my reason for living, as essential to my life as a hot shower or my morning cup of coffee. Extending yourself to those in need or working to make your community a healthier place to live goes beyond just being nice; these things allow you to act selflessly, expecting nothing in return. But you will gain something back: joy and self-worth.

As for my parents, who worked so hard their entire lives to make sure their family could be as comfortable as possible, they no longer worry about me, even as my high school peers graduate from college. They now understand my mission, see that I am happy, see the satisfaction I instill in others, too.

Even my parents get involved now, supporting charities like Habitat for Humanity and giving regularly to community-service organizations in their hometown.

In short, when you create a mini-miracle for someone in need, you are not doing what life requires you to do, but what your human soul allows you to do best. We all have a natural capacity to be kind and generous; this book will strengthen that innate skill so you can create the most powerful, most meaningful, most effective mini-miracles to make the world a better place and see your own life begin to change for the better.

Angel Power Rule #1

CREATE MIRACLES: CLIFFS NOTES–STYLE

*Don't wait for your "ship to come in," and feel angry
and cheated when it doesn't. Get going with something small.*

—IRENE KASSORLA, *GO FOR IT*

Create a mini-miracle. Read that phrase again and write it down. It is the foundation of kindness, my motive for writing this book, and my reason for living. It is the easiest and most effective way to make a significant, lasting difference in the world.

When we say the word "miracle," our minds concoct intimidating scenarios: rescuing a classroom of children from a burning building, raising millions of dollars to find a cure for cancer, planting thousands of fruit-bearing trees in the desert to feed a starving tribe. And if you're like most people, you think being a miracle worker takes lots of time, lots of

1

hard work, and possibly an act of God to be a one-person army, a life-saving, cure-finding, mentor-for-life saint.

The fact is, to create miracles and make a difference, all you have to do is devote fifteen minutes a day. In the same amount of time it takes to walk to the corner grocery store, you can change the world.

Change the World in Just Fifteen Minutes a Day?

If you're like me, you are always trying to find ways to save time by doing two errands at once or by taking advantage of services that perform time-consuming chores like laundry and grocery shopping. Just look at your appointment book or calendar. I bet your day is crammed with meetings, errands, and an indefinite number of tasks. Do you bring a laptop computer with you on the airplane so you can get some work done? Do you wonder how you've lived without a cellular phone? Or maybe you don't have time to wonder. Here's the point: There just don't seem to be enough hours in the day to accomplish everything you want to do. Time, if you really think about it, is your most precious commodity.

No matter how hectic our lives become, however, I believe that to be human is to want to contribute something positive to the world. Our capacity to be compassionate and help others is inborn. We want to help a sick child, clean up a littered park, raise money for a charitable cause we believe in. But with all of the chores and responsibilities we have, where can we possibly find time to do something positive for humanity and still maintain our busy lives?

Maybe at some moment in your life you "made the time." You fulfilled your need to give back to the world and volunteered, raised money for charity, or even got your hands and clothing dirty by planting trees in an inner-city garden. It felt great. Anyway, it was cheaper than paying $100 an hour to a therapist to tell you what you discovered for free: Being selfless made you a better person.

Then reality enters: family obligations, paperwork from the office, unpaid bills, perhaps a leaky roof. All of a sudden, your goal of recruiting one hundred people to participate in an AIDS walkathon fell off your list of priorities into a dark abyss, never to be seen or heard from again. "At least my intentions were good," you tell yourself.

Good intentions never get anything done. If I intended to wash the dishes one morning, and didn't, I'd still have a sinkful of dirty dishes. Taking responsibility and following through get the job done, not meaning well. The good news is that with technology making our lives quicker, easier, and more efficient, we can take a cue from the twenty-first century and make our philanthropic work quicker, easier, and more efficient as well.

In this book, you'll read the phrase "get the maximum amount done in the minimum amount of time." This is my work ethic. I do not believe in wasting time. And I certainly do not believe in achieving very little for a lot of hard work. That's what drove me to create fifteen-minute mini-miracles. Fifteen-minute miracles, or miracles Cliffs Notes–style, allow you to go beyond just being nice. They allow you to accomplish something concrete by helping someone in need or making your community a healthier place to live—without sacrificing a lot of your own time. You can change the world by embracing the Ten Rules of Angel Power to get the maximum amount done in the minimum amount of time and by committing fifteen minutes every single day to contribute something worthy to humanity.

I admit that this sounds like one of those unfounded claims from an infomercial touting an "amazing, ingenious product." And, as with those commercial spots, the only way to find out if my claim is true is to try it out yourself. In this case, however, you don't have to send four payments of $19.95.

It goes beyond writing a check to a charity. A fifteen-minute mini-miracle super-charges the idea: For example, instead of just writing a check, you can write a check to charity and double the amount in fifteen minutes without actually having to give more from your own checking account. You can even raise $1,000 for your favorite charity in fifteen minutes flat.

Over the last nine years, I've tested, perfected, and practiced more than one hundred of these mini-miracles. I think they're amazing—they've done so much to help others and improve my community, and they've made me a happier, better person, too.

Who or What Benefits?

By practicing fifteen-minute mini-miracles, you can

- help an elderly patient heal;
- help a child learn to read;

- donate $1,000 to charity without having to give a dime from your personal savings;
- save the life of a dying child;
- educate someone thousands of miles away during your lunch break;
- inspire a young woman to believe in herself.

Fifteen-minute mini-miracles are revolutionary. They're savvy and modern. They take full advantage of technology and the wealth of free information and resources available to us twenty-four hours a day, and turn our weaknesses into strengths—or, as I like to say, lemons into lemonade.

Change Your Life

And, as they say in those infomercials, that's not all, folks. Not only can you make a difference in just minutes a day, you'll get an added bonus if you act right now: No, you won't get washboard abs, but your life will change.

When you give a few minutes of your life each day to changing the world, your heart and soul open up. You find personal fulfillment. You gain self-worth. You learn valuable lessons that will help you succeed in the workplace, with your family, and in your personal life. You become a compassionate person not because you aspire to be one, but because your natural capacity to be kind shines through. And you inspire those around you to make a difference, too.

You'll also discover that the more that you self-lessly give, the better you'll feel about yourself and the world around you. The better you feel, the more you'll desire to change the world. The more you desire to change the world, the more tempting it will be to spend more than your daily fifteen minutes doing it. Pretty soon, devoting an entire weekend with your friends and family to building a Habitat for Humanity home won't sound time-consuming to you; it will be fun. After all, meaningful activities are what some of the best memories are made of.

A Review

Mini-miracles will make the world a better place, help those in need, and change your own life. This may sound like some new-agey idea to you, but I think there's nothing unusual about mixing the human need to make a difference with the time constraints and technology of the twenty-first century. Why shouldn't miracles evolve with the times?

At the end of each chapter in this book, you'll find ten proven fifteen-minute mini-miracles you can perform at the office, during your lunch hour, at home, on weekends, or right before you go to sleep. Take note of the mini-miracle ideas that interest you, and apply the inspiration and lessons you'll learn from the Ten Rules of Angel Power throughout the book. I guarantee that creating a daily mini-miracle will become a welcome and integral part of your life.

TEN MINI-MIRACLES
YOU CAN DO TO CHANGE YOUR WORLD

1. Donate your airline frequent-flier miles to a children's organization that helps sick and dying kids. Miracle Flights for Kids will accept your frequent-flier miles and use them to fly sick children to treatment centers and hospitals around the country. Call (702) 261-0494 or log on to www.miracleflights.com to donate your miles.

You can also donate your Northwest Airlines and United Airlines miles to benefit the Elizabeth Glaser Pediatric AIDS Foundation. Call United Mileage Plus Service Center at (800) 325-0041 or Northwest AirCares program at (800) 327-2881 to donate miles.

2. When children from the foster-family system are placed with a family, their clothing is usually transported in plastic trash bags. You can help by collecting used but good-condition suitcases from friends, family, and coworkers. Contact a local foster-family agency about donating luggage.

3. Here's a mini-miracle I do when I travel: I collect bottles of shampoo, conditioner, mouthwash, and bars of soap from hotels. (I'll even ask the front desk to collect a substantial amount from the supply closet for me, too.) When I return home after a vacation or lecture tour, I'll donate them to a local shelter.

4. If you're approached by a homeless person for money, it's your call if you want to give or not to give. Just don't just ignore or brush him aside. According to several homeless advocacy organizations, by at least making eye contact, you not

only acknowledge a homeless person's existence but you boost his self-esteem.

5. Put old and used cellular phones to work for the good of the community. Bell Atlantic Mobile will "recycle" your phones by reprogramming them to dial 911 at the touch of a button to help community safety patrols have direct access to police support. Call (914) 365-7535 or visit www.bam.com for more information.

6. Ever buy a stock on a "hot tip" only to watch it fizzle? Cut your losses, take a tax deduction, and support a worthy charity at the same time. The Nature Conservancy and Humane Society of the United States regard gifts of stocks and bonds as permanent investments in their critical work. You can donate to the Nature Conservancy by visiting www.tnc.org or to the Humane Society of the United States by calling (800) 808-7858.

7. Ready to embark on an adventure? Share the wonders of the world by participating in the Austin Center Post Card Project. Whether you're visiting towers of steel or meadows of green, let a group of men and women living with HIV and AIDS in the Washington, D.C., area

hear about your adventures around the country or abroad. Send your postcards to: The Austin Center for Health and Living, Whitman Walker Clinic, 1407 S Street, N.W., Washington, D.C., 20009.

8. Did you know that children with music education perform better in math and develop better problem-solving skills than children without music education? It's true. If you've got a musical instrument lying around your house from your high school days, like a violin, trumpet, or clarinet, donate it to the music education department at a local school. They will put the instrument to good use.

9. If you have a four-wheel-drive vehicle, inform your local hospital that you're willing to drive nurses and doctors to the hospital during fierce wintry weather.

10. Donate used golf clubs to the Clubs for Kids program sponsored by the Professional Golfers Association of America (PGA). The clubs will be used to introduce young people to golf who otherwise would not be able to afford to play. Write to the PGA, Box 109601, Palm Beach Gardens, Florida, 33410, for more information.

Angel Power Rule #2

SHATTER YOUR PERSONAL GLASS CEILING

*Some people believe it's a good idea to face
your fears. I usually feel that it's much healthier
to tie them up in a bag, drive out to the country,
chuck them out your window,
then drive home as fast as you can.*

— ELLEN DeGENERES

The path to making a difference in the world does not begin at the soup kitchen or volunteer center. It starts with facing your true feelings about helping others.

The reality is that most of us have an aversion to extending ourselves to others to the fullest extent. I'll even go so far as to say that many of us fear being altruistic.

It's important to acknowledge our true feelings about service and charity. Yes, helping others and working to improve your community are fulfilling, joyous acts. But if you feel, for example, that you do not have enough time or skills to contribute to a charity, then you create a personal glass ceiling that stops you from experiencing the pleasures and joys of altruism. In this chapter, you will find out how to shatter that personal glass ceiling into tiny pieces, allowing you to offer all that you are truly able to give to make your world a better place to live.

The Charitable Glass Ceiling

There are many fears each of us faces every day. Some children sleep at night with a light on; they fear the boogeyman will appear once the light goes out. College seniors who are about to leap (or, in most cases, be forced) into the real world fear they will not find a job, never be independent, and will never be able to pay back their massive college loans. Even powerful corporate CEOs fear that one day they'll make (or repeat) an awful decision that will harm the reputation and bottom line of the company. But we know better. Children grow up and no longer need a light to keep the boogeyman at bay; college students succeed in the real world; and CEOs can make landmark decisions that earn their companies millions of dollars. They persevere over their fears.

Many of us never know, let alone admit, that we fear being charitable. But it's fear that prevents you from giving to your full potential.

So what is preventing you from extending yourself to volunteerism and service? Ask yourself:

- Does working with sick or dying people scare me? Why?
- Do I feel like my life is so busy that I don't have time to spare for volunteerism?
- Do I think volunteer activities are competitive?
- Am I shy? Do I find volunteering with unfamiliar people in unfamiliar environments intimidating?
- Have I ever volunteered for an organization, disliked the experience, and never discussed my displeasure with the organization? Have I ever returned to volunteer again?
- Was I forced to do community-service work in school as part of a graduation requisite that left a bad image of volunteerism in my mind?

Now put this book down, walk over to a quiet place, and determine once and for all what is really holding you back from giving to your full potential. "I am afraid of people who are dying" or "I feel I have nothing worthy to contribute" are some fears I hear often. Once you determine what your fears are, it's easy to overcome them. There are no lengthy counseling sessions, medications, or barefoot walks across hot coals. The truth is that most fears of altruism are unfounded.

Following are the most common fears.

- I fear I will be more of a hindrance to an organization than an asset
- I fear I have nothing worthy to contribute
- I do not have enough time to volunteer
- I fear I will be pressured into making too much of a commitment
- I am afraid of sick or dying people

Isn't it ironic that an act of generosity that brings so much joy and self-worth to so many people can also stir up such fears in others? It's a shame that fear prevents people from seeing the joy in altruism. A fear that limits your ability to make a difference in the world will rob you of much that life has to offer. To achieve victory over fear, we must confront the invisible barrier that prevents us from creating Heaven on Earth and uncover the source that energizes this fear.

Understanding the Glass Ceiling

Often, our fear of making a difference in the lives of those in need or in our community results in the creation of a personal glass ceiling. The personal glass ceiling is not much different from the corporate glass ceiling many of us face in the workplace. The only difference is that the corporate glass ceiling is created by an employer or corporation, while the personal ceiling is created by us.

In the workplace, there are steps you might take to shatter the corporate glass ceiling, like devoting extra hours to a project proposal that eventually lands the big account, or taking evening college classes to learn invaluable job skills. The goal is to move up the corporate ladder right into that cushy corner office while gaining respect from your peers and the powers that be.

Some of you reading this book might be at the top of your career path, might be starting your own business, might be fulfilling your dream of working out of the comfort of your own home. Many of you have the most important career of all: raising children who will one day become compassionate, good-hearted citizens contributing to humanity and to the goodwill of the world. (I firmly believe that raising a family is the most important and time-consuming job of all.) You shattered your professional glass ceiling and now lead the work life you want to lead. Congratulations.

Still, you may fear helping others — it may even be news to you that you have this fear. (As my friend Melinda might say, "Denial ain't just a river in Egypt!") But if you've ever had your stomach turn the moment someone asked you to volunteer at a homeless shelter or take part in a charitable activity, that's not indigestion — it's fear.

"Oh, I'm not afraid to make a difference," another friend told me when she read the first draft of this book. But when we discussed what she was actually doing to make a difference in the world (not what she perceived she was contributing), considering the skills she had to offer, the discovery shocked her: She wasn't giving to her full potential.

Think of it this way. Let's say you hear about a great job opportunity in your field of expertise that pays an extraordinary amount of money. But you think it's going to be very competitive and you decide that you will not get the job. You do not bother applying, and weeks later, the job gets filled and you're still stuck at a job you loathe. For years afterward, you think, What if I had applied? What if I had gotten the job? What if . . .

Well, what *if* you have the ability to change the world and you don't because of some silly unfounded fear? So go. Take a chance. And confront your fears.

To shatter your personal glass ceiling, you need to recognize and confront whatever fear you have. First, let's debunk those common fears.

Fear #1:
I Fear I Will Be More of a Hindrance to an Organization than an Asset

---

In an episode of the television show *Ellen*, the lead character, Ellen Morgan, volunteers with a community-service group, Helping Hand, every spare minute she can offer. In one example of several volunteer activities she (gracelessly) performs, she calls potential donors for contributions. In Ellen's world, other volunteers successfully raise money while she comes up with zippo. Predictably, she gets frustrated by all the rejection. She reaches the boiling point: Ellen condescendingly scolds a potential donor over the telephone for not giving money to the organization. "Oh! Do you think you could give a whole penny? Or, maybe that's too much for you!! Boo, hoo!" Any chance that person is going to support Helping Hand in the near future? Don't count on it.

The volunteer director pulls her aside for a chat.

"I really do appreciate your coming here. But we're going to have to let you go," says the director.

"You're firing me?" questions Ellen. "But I'm a volunteer!"

"Yes, but we need the space that you're filling up."

Humorous, yes. Realistic, no. This is, however, a perfect example of the fear many of us have about volunteerism. We believe that we will be more of a hindrance than an asset, that our failure to provide any useful assistance to a charity will do more harm than good for the organization. This fear alone prevents a lot of people from getting involved with a worthy organization. And with good reason: Who wants to harm a charity?

But the facts don't support the fear. Reputable charitable organizations have systems in place to prevent volunteers from causing harm: providing proper training, and making sure the volunteer feels comfortable with a project, understands any instructions, and feels like part of the "team." At Earth 2000 National, I tried to create a warm environment where everyone felt appreciated (which they were) and felt part of the solution (which they were). And, of course, I never brought in volunteers if there was nothing to do.

Miracle Worker: Diane Bock

It all started on April 29, 1992. How could you watch the riots in South Central Los Angeles and not feel devastated, horrified, and helpless at the violence and mayhem? That was the exact sentiment of Diane Bock as she watched the riots from her comfortable suburban San Diego home. "What," she asked herself over and over again, "can I do to alleviate this problem?" How could this homemaker with an infant child possibly help to end racial ignorance?

She realized that one person *could* be the answer. "Barriers have gone up between people brick by brick, and that's how they must come down: one brick at a time." This could be a solution, Diane believed, to ending racial hatred and ignorance in Los Angeles.

To make her dream a reality, she created Community Cousins, a nonprofit organization that brings families of different backgrounds together to "connect." The key, according to Diane, is to encourage families to develop friendships out of shared interests and to get together on their own terms—not to force them to interact. They share children's clothing and toys, attend picnics, play baseball games, have holiday gatherings, and host block parties on a regular basis. "The material things are actually secondary, but they provide a good mechanism for contact and after only a few encounters the sparks of friendship begin to ignite, especially with kids."

And kids change for the better. In many cases, children who never interacted with children of other races are no longer in shock when they see each other: different colors of skin, different shapes of eyes, and different hair colors are celebrated as something special. In fact, children who once considered racial stereotypes and slurs as the norm consider them "bogus" today.

As these families bond and learn from each other, Diane spends most of her time keeping Community Cousins going. She admits that a lot of people feel her idea is a good solution, but many do not get involved. Why? Some people still think they can never be part of the solution. But that's exactly what Diane thought the night of the Los Angeles riots. After helping more than two hundred families build relationships that break down the barriers of racial ignorance, the results speak for themselves.

What could a suburban homemaker with a newborn baby contribute to heal the racial wounds of downtown Los Angeles? Plenty. Diane overcame her fear of not being part of the solution and began her crusade to heal America.

Here's something you can do. The next time you're watching the evening news and feel horrified or heartbroken over a story, do something. It could be as simple as writing a check, sharing the story with a neighbor, or locating a community organization to volunteer with. You could even host a neighborhood block party to discuss issues facing your community. Just don't accept things the way they are. Remember, doing something, even an act you may consider insignificant, is being part of the solution.

Fear #2:
I Fear I Have Nothing Worthy to Contribute

I'm going to set the record straight. Every single human being on the face of this planet has something positive and worthy to contribute to society, to humanity, and definitely to a charitable organization.

Remember the quotation from Albert Schweitzer? "Example is not the main thing in influencing others. It is the only thing." Now practice what he preached.

Think hard about an adverse situation you had to overcome. How did you persevere and become a stronger individual? There are other young people out there who are dealing with the same issues you faced as a young person. The world is a tougher place to grow up in than it was even five years ago. Too many kids do not have mentors, lack adult guidance, and they need your help. You don't have to set up a home for at-risk youth, but you can mentor one young person. It can be a neighborhood teen or a child from a local at-risk youth organization. (If you want how to mentor a child, please see the mentoring section later on in "I Believe Children Are the Present," page 185.

What's the greatest thing you can contribute to the world? Look in the mirror and you'll find your answer.

What Can You Offer?

Still think you have nothing worthy to contribute to a charitable organization? The truth is you have many, many talents to offer, perhaps too many even to write down on a piece of paper. There are people all around you who are in total awe of your talents, unable to comprehend the extraordinary things you accomplish every day. The reason you feel like you have nothing to offer is simple: Your own special skills are second nature to you. "Oh, this is a skill? I could do it in my sleep." Exactly.

What are your special talents and skills? What do you have to offer? Answer the questions as honestly as possible.

- When was the last time someone came to you with a problem? Were you able to offer a solution? What was that problem and what steps did you take to solve it? You can use your problem-solving skills to help a young person in need by volunteering at a youth crisis telephone hot line.
- Do you have any musical talents? When I was a teenager, I studied the violin and piano as a hobby. Four times a year, I would play at charity dinners and at senior-citizens centers during the holiday season. You can also volunteer at a charitable organization by playing at its fund-raising events.
- Look around the house and gather anything you made yourself, like a piece of pottery, a handmade Christmas card, an intricately wrapped present. Do you have a "hands-on" talent? During the holiday season, charities need

people with crafts skills to help with seasonal fund-raisers, such as wrapping presents at the shopping mall or creating items for a crafts sale.

- When is the last time you fixed something yourself? What did you fix and how did you learn how to it? Public parks, homeless shelters, youth centers, animal shelters, and other charities that use buildings and permanent fixtures as part of their work can utilize your talents to maintain and keep up their property.

- When was the last time you won an award? (If you have to go back to your high school days, then pull out that dusty yearbook.) Why did you win that award? If you won the science fair in high school, for example, you can volunteer your time at a local school to help organize a science fair, judge one, or even mentor a young person's project for an existing event.

Have you ever been on a swim team? You could volunteer to teach swimming to kids at the YMCA. Do you knit? Make hats and scarves for a local clothing drive. Are you a great shopper who always finds terrific discounts? Volunteer to shop with previously homeless women who are about to enter the workplace; show them how to stretch each dollar to create a new wardrobe.

Do you see how a seemingly insignificant skill like swimming, knitting, or shopping can have a significant impact on others and your community? This is the idea behind fifteen-minute mini-miracles. You don't have to lead massive movements to make a difference. A diving lesson here . . . a homemade sweater there . . . a trip to the shopping mall . . . *that's* changing the world.

An Exercise: Ordinary to Extraordinary

Here are some ordinary tasks, using ordinary skills, that many of us tackle every day. How can you use these ordinary skills to create mini-miracles? To get you going, I've offered my own ideas, but please don't limit yourself to what I suggest. There are many ways to use ordinary skills to help others.

1. Recording television shows. If you can program your VCR, you can help a charitable organzation. Many advocacy organizations, whether they work to protect our oceans or lobby Congress to increase spending in education, can use your

help. You can record your local television news when relevant local stories can assist their national agenda.

2. Gardening. In the fall, offer to plant spring flower bulbs at local hospitals, schools, playgrounds, parks, or public buildings to help brighten up your community. If you want, you can invite a class of young kids to learn the basics of gardening while they help you improve their school.

3. Dog training. Is dog training really an ordinary skill? If you can housebreak Rex and teach him to sit, lie down, speak, or stay, then you'd come in mighty handy at the local animal shelter. Canines with a crash course in discipline are more likely to be adopted than animals with little or no obedience.

4. Photography. While you may not be the next Ansel Adams, perhaps your friends and colleagues have admired your talent behind the camera. If so, offer to create "before," "during," and "after" snapshots of the building process of a Habitat for Humanity home. The pictures will be bound and given to the new homeowner, and the affiliate building the home can use the pictures in its newsletter for fundraising purposes.

Now it's your turn. What ordinary skill can you offer that'll make a difference?

Fear #3:
I Do Not Have Enough Time to Volunteer

Another reason many people feel reluctant to volunteer is a lack of time. While all of us have at least fifteen minutes a day to create a mini-miracle, most of us do not have the luxury of hours of time to offer to a charitable organization.

The Points of Light Foundation (see Resource Guide for contact information) has a complete directory of volunteer centers all over the country that are trained to locate volunteer activities for busy people. In my hometown, I'm a member of Greater DC Cares, the largest coordinator of volunteer activities in the Washington, D.C., metropolitian area. Every month, DC Cares sends out a monthly calendar of volunteer opportunities that list specific dates, times, and descriptions of dozens of interesting volunteer activities. I can reference the calendar when I know I have a free weekend coming up and sign up with the volunteer activity of my choice.

If you already have a favorite organization you volunteer with, it's important never to be inundated with tasks that you are doing for them. While that may sound like I am advising you to be selfish, I'm not. I'm advising you to be "self-full." This is a preventive measure to ensure you are at your peak ability to be happy; if you're not happy, you cannot create mini-miracles that are meaningful and effective. So how do you prevent being overwhelmed by a charitable organization? Here are a few suggestions:

1. Try to work in teams when volunteering so the burden won't rest solely on your shoulders.

2. Say "no" when appropriate and stick to it.

3. Recognize as early as possible if you are being overwhelmed by an organization and be vocal about it. To avoid feeling trapped, remember all your other good deeds and simply say, "I can't get involved right now. I wouldn't be able to give enough time to make this project succeed."

When my good friend Kathryn helped a kind woman rescue feral cats so they could be spayed or neutered, she didn't recognize early enough that the woman was overwhelming her.

When the woman began to depend too much on Kathryn, calling her late at night and pleading for large sums of money to pay overdue vet bills (one bill came to $1,000 for just one cat's consultation), she didn't know what to do. As the calls intensified late into the night and as Kathryn started to screen her calls and get anxious every time the phone rang, I could see her growing discontent, not just with the woman, but with charity in general. One day, seeing how sad she was, my advice to Kathryn was blunt: Stop volunteering with this woman. I helped Kathryn see how this woman was disrespectful to her; she followed my advice and her life returned to normal.

How to Say No

All right, maybe it's not in your vocabulary to say no. It's not nice, it's disrespectful, and you really don't want to hurt anybody's feelings.

That's fine. In fact, it's probably better to avoid saying "no" when there are far more effective and easier ways to be assertive to those who make unfair requests or demands of you. Here is my advice on saying no effectively—sometimes without actually having to utter the word "no":

1. Saying "I will not" or "I have decided not to" emphasizes the fact that your decision is already made and is not up for discussion.

2. Make sure your body language matches your verbal reaction to a request. When you turn down a request, make sure you shake your head, too.

3. Don't say you're sorry. That compromises the strength of saying no and gives the impression of apologizing to unreasonable demands.

4. Be brief when stating your reason for saying no. Lengthy, detailed explanations can give the other person ammunition for arguing with your decision.

5. Finally, just say "no." It has power (especially if you rarely say it) and is less ambiguous than saying "I'm not sure."

Fear #4:
I Am Afraid of Sick and Dying People

When I was a teenager, I volunteered regularly at a local AIDS hospice. Volunteering around those suffering from advanced stages of HIV infection was never an issue with me, in large part because I grew up around the hospital where my father worked as a doctor.

It is, however, a real concern for many people. If you have a fear of working around those who are ill or suffering from a life-threatening disease, then it's important for you to determine if helping the sick and dying is right for you. I'm not saying you should never make an effort to confront and over-come your fear, but you should do so on your own time. It would be inappropriate to use a volunteer activity at a hospice or hospital as an opportunity to overcome your fear of working around dying people.

If you cannot overcome your fear of sick and dying people, but you still want to help at a hospice or treatment center, consider volunteering your time on an administrative or fund-raising project. Many medical organizations depend on volunteers to help run the office, raise money, or deal with the day-to-day tasks that keep them running.

Beyond Fear

To be honest, all of my successes in my personal, professional, and charitable ventures were direct results of my ability to face my fears and shatter my personal glass ceiling.

By shattering my fears, I feel free. Problems are manageable, I'm organized, and I have direction in my life. Writing this reminds me of the *Saturday Night Live* skit in which comedian Kevin Nealon reads a news report that a diet high in fat is bad for you. He goes on to say that this "shocking" news report is from the medical journal *Duh*.

That's how I feel about shattering my fears. Faced with a problem? The solution is obvious. A charity needs a new angle on a project? Not a problem. Want to do something to bring some interest back into your career? Give me five minutes and a cup of coffee, I'll think of something. Everything is from the *Duh* level of thinking. It's obvious. And it will become obvious to you, too.

Remember the snowstorms of 1993? In Pennsylvania that year, snowfalls were so common that meteorologists measured snow by the foot, not the inch.

I was so bored sitting at home with nothing to do during the '93 storms that I spent lots of time reading every piece of mail (including junk mail) that had arrived before the snowstorm hit. I knew others in my area were most likely reading their mail, too.

The next year, when I was preparing a direct-mail appeal for Earth 2000, I separated the letters by zip code, that were going to areas normally hit by snow. If the forecast for Connecticut, for example, predicted snow in five days, the letters were mailed that day to members in Connecticut. My philosophy was that if our members received their mail before a snowstorm, they would read the newsletter and fund-raising appeal more closely because of the sheer boredom of being trapped in their homes.

Normally, if a nonprofit organization's mailing receives a two percent return from its members, it's declared a success. By coordinating our mailings with the weather, however, we received an astonishing 23.5 percent return—all because I was able to get an idea from a situation most people would have seen as a negative. I applied the lessons I learned from shattering my personal glass ceiling to my organization and turned lemons into lemonade.

When you face your fears, you'll begin to see a world of possibility. You'll become a happier person, with purpose. Your confidence will be higher than ever. And, most important, you will be able to truly make a difference in the life of another person, you will be able to make your community a healthier place to live, and you will contribute to the well-being of our planet.

Ten Mini-Miracles
You Can Do to Change Your World

1. Send your used holiday cards to St. Jude's Ranch for Children. This nonprofit residence for abused and neglected children gives kids the opportunity to earn extra money by recycling the fronts of used greeting cards. Proceeds from the card sales benefit the facility. Send your cards to 100 St. Jude's Street, Boulder City, Nevada, 89005.

2. Help a teenager at a youth center write his or her first resume; lay out the resume on the computer and print out copies on good-quality paper. Post a sign on the community bulletin board at the local YMCA offering your resume assistance to a young person ready to enter corporate America.

3. If your company usually pays for first- or business-class airline travel, offer to fly coach and request that the savings be donated to charity instead.

4. Mary Tyler Moore, Cindy Crawford, and Kim Basinger are just a few of Hollywood's elite who have spoken out against wearing fur. If you endorse fur-free living, and would like to put your old fur coat to good use, you can recycle it and support medical research at the same time. McCrory Bears, a family business in Massachusetts, will recycle your old fur into cuddly teddy bears and donate the proceeds to the National Kidney Foundation. Contact McCrory Bears, P.O. Box 305, Rockport, Massachusetts 01966.

5. When you make a contribution to a charity that provides you with a postage-paid business reply envelope, add a stamp anyway. This saves the charity money, about fifty cents for postage and handling, which can be used for its programs instead.

6. The next time you read an inspiring article in the newspaper about a local community-service group, clip it out. Send the article to the com-

munity relations department of a local company you do business with and include a note saying, "I think it would be great if you supported this charity."

7. If you're a member of an art museum, donate your free guest passes to a local school. The passes can be given to art students who would otherwise be unable to pay the admission fee.

8. Nominate an extraordinary person for a community-service award. Contact the Giraffe Project, an organization that recognizes people for "sticking their necks out for the common good," so that a worthy person can receive a Giraffe Award. Call (360) 221-7989 for a nomination kit. The Giraffe Project offers support and services to award winners and helps them see their philanthropic dreams come true.

9. When you're finished reading *Heaven on Earth*, donate it to a school or public library so others can get inspired and take action, too.

10. Collect your spare change for a whole month in a jar. At the end of the month, have it counted at a bank that has a change-counting machine. Send a check in the amount of the change to a worthy charity.

Angel Power Rule #3
U.B.U. (YOU BE YOU)

Think wrongly if you please,
but in all cases think for yourself.

— DORIS LESSING

Marian Wright Edelman wrote in her book *The Measure of Our Success* that "it is utterly exhausting being Black in America—physically, mentally, and emotionally." As an Asian-American, I can relate.

Until my senior year in high school, I had never been attacked for being one of a handful of minority students attending a predominantly white school. I didn't think racism was a problem in 1995.

One morning, however, I discovered how naive I was: My locker was smashed open and racial slurs were scrawled all over the inside. I was shocked. When I complained to the school principal, I was confident action would be swift and immediate because I assumed any public school—especially in

1995—would not tolerate hate. Instead, justice was not served; the school would not fix my locker—"to save money"—and instead provided me with a shelf in the hallway to store my books. I was furious.

When I talked about the incident with a friend, he replied, "That's weird. You're the whitest Asian I know."

"What is *that* supposed to mean?" I asked.

"You know. You talk, dress, and act just like the rest of us," he said.

"The rest of us?"

Because I spoke fluent English and "blended in," he felt I should have been "tolerated." He brought up another Asian-American student in my school who had immigrated to the U.S. as a child and spoke broken English (to me, his speaking two languages was far more impressive than if he had spoken just one). That student was taunted, singled out, and spoken to in a condescending manner by other students and teachers every single day. I guess he didn't act "white" enough and I should have counted my lucky stars that I had to tolerate "only" one act of hatred.

Surprisingly, the racist slurs and the uncaring school didn't bother me as much as the comment that I was "the whitest Asian" my friend knew. That comment raised some serious questions for me. Had I been living the life that I truly wanted to lead or was I unknowingly denying my true purpose by trying to fit in? I had some thinking to do.

To figure out who I really was, I decided to write a mission statement for myself, as I had already done for my organization. This exercise proved to be of real value. My mission statement spelled out three goals. First, I wanted to show people of all ages and races that it truly is possible for one person to change his or her part of the world. Second, by being not an Asian-American activist but rather an activist who happens to be Asian-American, I hoped to be a role model to young Asian-Americans without having to scream at the top of my lungs, "I am Asian and proud of it." My last goal was to seek personal fulfillment by helping others. I wanted to be an "entrepreneur" of altruism.

With this book, the hundreds of letters and E-mails I receive from young Asian-Americans, and the fact I wake up every morning looking forward to what each day will bring me, I am fulfilling the three goals outlined in my mission statement. Every year or so, usually on New Year's Day, I alter the mission statement to reflect my ever-changing vision of myself and the world around me.

I owe so much to the exercise of creating a mission statement. It may seem hokey at first, but once you create a standard that is uniquely yours—not that of your peers and not one based on preconceived notions about your age, race, sex, or others' visions of you as "the whitest Asian person" they know—you may see how a mission statement can provide much-needed guidance in your life, too.

An Exercise: Who Are You?

We're bombarded every day with messages from advertisers, the media, our friends, our families, telling us what we should and shouldn't think. One moment we believe passionately in gun control, and the next moment we think every child should have his or her very own customized automatic water pistol. But we need to ignore these messages and follow what our hearts tell us.

What do you believe in? What do you truly feel passionate about?

To find the mission that best fits you, consider these questions:

1. What social issue do you feel most passionate about (e.g., the environment, AIDS awareness, finding a cure for cancer, reducing crime)? Once you determine what general issue you feel passionate about, try to narrow your focus. For example, if you care about the environment, a more specific cause might be conservation of our beaches or the protection of forests in your state.

2. To which charitable organization have you given the most financial support over the past two years? The charitable organization to which you give the most financial support may not have the mission you feel most passionate about. Even though the largest of my donations go to Habitat for Humanity, and even though I support their work, I still consider the protection of animals and our environment the issues I feel most passionate about. It's important not to not confuse how much you give financially with what your own mission is.

3. How would you describe yourself politically: conservative, moderate, liberal, or independent? Your political affiliation can mean a lot more than just how you vote in local, state, and national elections; it can help you create a mission. If you consider yourself a Democrat, you may believe in

increasing funds for education or protecting our environment. If you consider yourself a Republican, you may feel a strong need for less government in our lives. Then again, with party lines blurring, you may be a moderate Republican supporting tax reform and increased spending for the arts. However you feel, your political affiliation could provide some valuable insight into your mission.

4. Would you rather support a grassroots organization or an established national charity? If you think local organizations can have a greater impact on the world by attacking the roots of problems at the local level, then you should work with one. On the other hand, if you think an organization that has millions of members and millions of dollars in its coffers can change the world more effectively, then you should support that charity.

5. Do you prefer working at a hands-on or at an adminstrative level? There are two very different ways to volunteer at a nonprofit organization. Some prefer working on an administrative level, writing text for a Web site, for example, or entering names into a database, or proofreading a monthly newsletter. Some prefer working with their hands, peeling vegetables at the soup kitchen, say, or planting trees in a city park.

Take a moment to think about your answers. Some of these questions may be completely irrelevant to helping you define your mission, but others will probably be useful. It's up to you to decide what you feel passionate about. Forget what celebrities are preaching as the hot cause of the moment and ignore the pile of fund-raising appeals overflowing in your mailbox. What do *you* want to do? How do *you* want to create Heaven on Earth?

Writing Your Mission Statement

A mission statement is uniquely yours, allowing you to focus on what truly matters to you and guiding you in your mini-miracle work ahead.

Once you decide upon your mission, write it down in a one- or two-sentence statement. Find a business card and turn it over. On the blank side, write a general statement like:

"I want to build affordable housing for people in need."

"I want to mentor children in my community."

"I want to work for the protection of animals."

"I want to raise awareness of breast cancer."

Don't be *too* general, though. Writing something like "I want to save humanity" won't work. You need to be specific enough to point yourself on the road to action.

Keep this business card in your wallet, your organizer, or framed above your desk to serve as a daily reminder of your work here on Earth.

Your Annual Platform

In the spring of 1998, I teamed up with Miss America 1998, Kate Shindle, in New York City to help present the *react* magazine Take Action Awards to six extraordinary young people. These young "reactors" were leading their own charitable organizations and making a big difference in their communities.

After the awards ceremony, I confessed something to Miss America. No, it wasn't a secret infatuation. What I told her was that I had no idea what the Miss America program was about.

I had always assumed that the Miss America contest was just a beauty pageant—all fluff and no substance. But as it turned out, I had made a judgment without knowing the facts. The Miss America program, as Kate explained, provides more than $32 million in awards and scholarships to young women nationally every year. It also gives the reigning Miss America the opportunity to travel around the country to speak with civic organizations, schools, and government leaders about an issue that is close to her heart—her platform statement. Kate's platform was AIDS awareness, with an emphasis on young people.

Kate's platform inspired me to create my own annual platform to strengthen my mission statement. My personal mission statement listed general goals; it needed refinement. The platform statement immediately brought focus to my work for the year; 1998, I decided, would be the year I helped Habitat for Humanity.

Sticking to my platform, I was able to raise more than $64,000 for Habitat for Humanity and built homes in Baltimore, Maryland, and Little Rock, Arkansas, as well as help with plans to sponsor more homes on the West Coast. I owe it all to my platform.

I've also tried to apply my platform to my work and personal life whenever I can.

Because my platform for 1998 was to raise money for Habitat for Humanity, I decided to include a

provision for corporate giving in my business con-
tracts. When I signed with Pocket Books to publish
Heaven on Earth, I took the unusual step of inviting
my publisher to donate a portion of the proceeds
from the sale of this book to Habitat for Humanity.
The request took very little of my time and will raise
lots of money for a good cause.

An annual platform statement focuses your mission statement. It clearly defines what you want to
do in a given year to further your mission. If your
mission statement is to, say, protect the environment, your platform might be to plant trees in your
community. It's still a general statement, but it gives
you a place to begin.

You can use my annual platform for 1998 as a
model for creating your own: "For 1998, I will raise
money for Habitat for Humanity International of
Americus, Georgia." Do you see how this is still a
general statement? I didn't mention how much I
was going to raise, or how many homes I planned
on sponsoring. That's intentional. If I stated that my
goal was to raise $50,000, and I "only" ended up
raising $10,000, I'd dwell on the $40,000 deficit and
feel frustrated. Ten thousand dollars is still an awful
lot of money, an accomplishment anyone should be

proud of. But by not setting a lofty goal, I did not restrict my ability to raise money. I actually ended up surpassing my expectations.

Think about how you'd like to focus your mission. Once you settle on your annual platform, get a piece of paper and write it down. Your platform statement will guide you in your work for the year.

Miracle Worker: Michael Crisler

Michael Crisler was ten years old in 1999. In that brief time, he's endured five operations (with thirteen more ahead of him) to correct a rare condition called Treacher Collins syndrome, a birth defect that prevents the bones in his face from developing normally. One year he had a rib removed from his body so doctors could construct ears for him; the previous year, they removed another rib to build eye sockets. Despite these painful procedures, don't feel sorry for him. Instead, help him help others.

Michael's mission, since the age of six, has been to help others rather than to try to fit in. Despite his rare disease and painful and frequent surgeries, Michael's been raising money for other people who "have...a tougher life." He's raised money for children's hospitals and for disaster victims. He's collected toys for children who lost everything in natural disasters. He's never felt sorry for himself. He just wants to help others.

One day in 1995, when his mother drove him to to school, Michael was horrified to learn on the radio that hundreds of people were hurt in the Oklahoma City bombing. He was especially moved by news that children died in the tragedy. "I felt really sad and I didn't know what to do. When I saw a fireman carrying a child out of the building, I just knew I had to help," recalls Michael. He jumped into action and decided to raise money for the bombing victims.

"My mom suggested a bowlathon," he said. Michael agreed that would be a terrific fund-raiser and he recruited forty people to participate; more than three hundred sponsors gave money for each frame bowled.

At first, Michael's fund-raising goal for the event was $20,000. "I supported the idea," says Michael's mother, Gayle, who also suffers from Treacher Collins syndrome, "but I asked Michael if he knew how much $20,000 is. He looked back at me and said, 'Well, we have enough good people that I don't need to worry about that.'" Gayle was able to talk him down to a $10,000 goal.

Michael didn't raise $10,000. He raised $27,000. As the Denver community read in the newspaper about his amazing fund-raising feat, they donated more money, bringing the grand total up to $37,000. This was the largest cash contribution to help the Oklahoma City bombing victims from anyone, let alone a child.

Today, Michael's goal is to "raise a million dollars before I'm a teenager." He's raising money to support a number of charities dear to his heart, like the Children's Miracle Network, and he's also continuing to raise money for the Oklahoma City bombing victims. He's so good at fund-raising that the governor of Colorado put him in charge of a statewide "168 Pennies" campaign; people are asked to donate 168 pennies, "one for each person who died in the blast," explains

Michael. He's already raised $70,000 and no one doubts he'll reach his million-dollar goal.

Recently, Michael attended a ceremony in Oklahoma City to honor the victims. A woman who had survived but had permanent physical scars all over her face was still traumatized by the bombing and overwhelmed by the ceremony. Michael saw that her self-esteem was shot and walked up to her, looked right into her eyes, and said, "Don't worry about it. You look okay to me."

Michael's mission in life is to help others, despite his rare condition. He doesn't view himself as someone who is disabled, but as an example of what people can do if they put their minds and energy into making a difference. He focuses on a goal and creates a plan of action to reach that goal. Even when he reaches his goal, Michael doesn't dwell on his astonishing achievement. "He enjoys raising money, but when he's done, he's done. He moves on to the next project," says his mother.

Michael's story is a powerful example how a platform statement works. When he started to raise money for Oklahoma City victims, he created a platform to help them, focusing on his goal of raising $10,000. He ended up raising more than three times that amount. And each year as he continues to raise funds on behalf of others, his goal increases—it is now up to one million dollars.

Michael is a gutsy and savvy kid; he wouldn't agree to let me interview him unless I promised I'd invite each and every one of you reading this book to help him reach his million-dollar goal. Please see the resource guide in the back if you'd like to help Michael.

A Memorandum of Understanding

Michael Crisler raised $37,000 by using a memorandum of understanding to help him focus on his goal. What is a memorandum of understanding? It's the secret to accomplishing big mini-miracles.

I developed the idea of using a memorandum of understanding in my mini-miracle work when business partners from my noncharitable work required me to sign them. I saw how they worked and I decided to use them in my own efforts.

A memorandum of understanding is a great way to keep yourself focused on a goal. We all lead busy lives, and mine is probably no busier than yours. To keep myself organized and all parties on track, I require my business partners and myself to sign a memorandum of understanding that outlines the goals and deadlines of our business arrangement. I don't know how I've lived without one. Less complicated than an actual contract, a memorandum keeps both parties focused, prevents one party from exploiting another, and forces everyone to meet deadlines to avoid agreed-upon penalties. Everyone is efficient because of a piece of paper.

I use the same memorandums of understanding in my charitable work. The only difference is that there is only one party involved: me. Let's say I want to raise funds on behalf of a charity that fits my mission statement and my annual platform. If I plan to organize a small fund-raiser each month, I will draft a personal memorandum of understanding at the beginning of each month.

A mini-miracle memorandum of understanding outlines a very specific goal, when you intend to accomplish it, and what the penalty will be if the goal is not met by your deadline. The penalty, by the way, should never be severe; don't beat yourself up.

Let's say your mission statement is to help economically disadvantaged people and your platform for the year is to collect good-quality clothing. In November, you decide to collect one hundred jackets at your workplace for the local Salvation Army. You determine that fifteen minutes every morning in the office for the whole month will get you to this goal. To make sure you get there, you might draft and sign a personal memorandum of understanding along these lines:

A Memorandum of Understanding

The parties in this memorandum are [your name] (YN) and The Salvation Army (TSA) of Washington, D.C.

1. YN will collect one hundred good-quality winter jackets for TSA.

2. YN will deliver one hundred good-quality winter jackets to TSA no later than 12:00 P.M. on December 1, 1998.

3. TSA will distribute the jackets to those in need.

4. If YN fails to collect one hundred good-

quality jackets, he will deliver the total number collected by December 1, 1998, anyway. If YN does not meet at least 50 percent of the goal, YN will be penalized. The penalty for YN will be a whole month without chocolate.

Your Signature
Date

Post the memorandum of understanding in a visible place, like your refrigerator or the bulletin board next to your desk. You can tell a friend, or a loved one, about your memorandum so he or she can help you stay on top of your promise. It will be a daily, weekly, or monthly reminder of what you promised yourself to do.

A memorandum of understanding is not meant to be a declaration of some lofty, impossible goal you set for yourself. If you think one hundred jackets are too much but think ten jackets are reasonable, then write down ten jackets as your goal.

Remember that this is only a sample memorandum; it can be used as a model for any mini-miracle project. You can write a memorandum of understanding at the beginning of each month and give yourself thirty days to accomplish it, committing fifteen minutes each morning to reach that goal. That's twelve projects a year that take only minutes a day to do. Or you can write a memorandum of understanding at the beginning of the week with the end of the week as your deadline. You'll have to find what works for you.

Isn't a memorandum of understanding just busy-work?

I thought so until I saw how effective it was in helping me reach my goals. You don't need to write one if you plan on, say, changing an elderly neighbor's lightbulb. But if you draft one for bigger mini-miracle efforts, like collecting winter jackets, you'll see first-hand how integral it can be to the success of your project.

Emulate, Don't Imitate

People are surprised to learn that I do not think we should have role models. I do believe, however, we should look up to people and emulate, not imitate, those we admire.

The question I'm asked most often in my travels is, Which person has had the greatest influence on my life? Was it a world-famous humanitarian? My parents? A teacher who inspired me at an early age to get involved? Nope. It's Martha Stewart. That's right, the same woman who showed America how to line our kitchen cabinets with pretty fabrics—just so that when people snoop around they can think to themselves, My God, these shelves way up here at the tippy top are gorgeous.

Well, it's not just Martha Stewart. In addition to the queen of domesticity, Fox chairman Rupert Murdoch and humanitarian Albert Schweitzer are my personal inspirations. I admit these are odd choices for a teenager to admire, to study, to look up to for guidance and inspiration. But at a very early age, I began to develop a method of learning that was peculiarly my own. I would find exciting, interesting people who were leaders in their respective fields and emulate what they did best. But at all costs, I avoided imitating them.

I studied the work of Albert Schweitzer to create a firm ethical foundation for myself. This foundation keeps me true to my beliefs, whether they concern the protection of the environment, advocating the rights of animals, or promising to give at least 10 percent of my earnings to charitable organizations every year.

Rupert Murdoch taught me business skills. I read books and magazine articles about him and kept track of programs and franchises he personally oversaw and their successes and failures. Although I do not necessarily model myself on him in other ways, I did learn how to stand up for myself in a cutthroat business world and make wise financial decisions. With the lessons on ethics I learned from Schweitzer, and the effective business tactics I picked up from Murdoch, I was ready to conquer the world. Well, at least I thought I was.

Enter Martha Stewart. When I was sixteen years old, I was getting more media attention than any teenager should receive. So much so that the inevitable media backlash began to occur. No longer did editorials praise my work as a young person, but portrayed me as a rebellious teen out to cause trouble for adults. Radio personalities mocked me and would place prank calls to my home during morning "drive time" shows. I was even in the *National Enquirer.* The criticism was annoying and, worst of all, it was personal.

My good friend Melissa Hicks led me to Martha. Melissa is an atypical Martha Stewart fan. With brightly colored hair in shades of purple, pink, and green—it changes weekly—silver metallic moon boots, and a very colorful wardrobe that sometimes makes me wish I *was* colorblind, Melissa never misses an episode of *Martha Stewart Living*. Naturally, I had to see what all this fuss was over Martha. The more I watched, the more I found Martha Stewart the person, not the personality, fascinating. I found her persistence in her belief that domesticity can be a celebrated art form intriguing, especially in the face of all her detractors.

At the public library, I printed out scores of articles about Martha Stewart from mainstream and trade publications. I watched her television show. I read two years' worth of her magazine, *Martha Stewart Living*, cover to cover. I tracked her television talk show appearances and set my VCR to record them. I spent hours on the Internet reading unauthorized Web sites that were shrines to Martha Stewart, and those that were shrines to "people who hate Martha Stewart."

I came away with an interesting lesson from my experience with Martha: If you believe in your message no matter what, no amount of criticism can hurt you. In fact, it's the reason she succeeds at what she does. She's been criticized, mocked, parodied, but she charges right ahead. It's a simple message, granted. But it was a powerful one for me, perhaps life-changing.

I do not want to be Albert Schweitzer, Rupert Murdoch, or Martha Stewart. I want to be Danny Seo. But what I was able to learn from these three unique individuals were life lessons that helped me create a life that is my own.

Get inspired by someone you admire, learn something, and use that lesson to change your life and the world around you.

TEN MINI-MIRACLES
YOU CAN DO TO CHANGE YOUR WORLD

1. Because thousands of children and senior citizens hurt themselves by slipping on ice each year during the winter months, you can prevent accidents by throwing rock salt or deicing mixture on the sidewalk in front of your home.

2. Donate newspapers to an animal shelter. They will be shredded and used as bedding for rescued homeless cats and dogs.

3. Donate a health club guest pass to a local school; ask the school to reward the student who improves the most academically with the free pass.

4. At the end of the year, don't toss old calendars into the trash. The Sonoma County affiliate of Friends Outside, a nonprofit organization that serves prison inmates and their families, uses old calendars to create decorative boxes. Send your calendars to Friends Outside, P.O. Box 3905, Santa Rosa, California, 95402.

5. Bring voter registration forms to work and leave them in a conspicuous place.

6. When people make the transition from shelters to permanent homes, you can help them furnish their new quarters. Donate clean furniture in decent condition to a charitable collection agency like Goodwill Industries or the Salvation Army. People who receive furnishings choose the furniture that pleases them, which allows them to decorate to suit their personal tastes.

7. Children throughout the world are benefiting from the generosity of American Airlines passengers in a program called Change for Good. On all overseas flights on American Airlines,

passengers are given the opportunity to donate unwanted foreign coins to support UNICEF (the United Nations Children's Fund), which helps improve the lives of children in more than 160 countries around the world. The next time you fly American Airlines International Flagship Service, you can unload a pocketful of lire, yen, or francs and help kids at the same time.

8. In the month of February, bring a pair of good-quality used shoes to any Kenneth Cole retail store and save 20 percent off a new pair of Kenneth Cole shoes. All shoes are given to Help USA, a homeless relief organization. For more information, call (800) KEN-COLE or Help USA at (800) 311-7999.

9. Shop at a grocery store that donates a percentage of the register receipts to support local schools. Collect your receipts and drop them off in the appropriate box at the supermarket.

10. If you've got any scrap metal, such as a junked brass bed or wiring from a home renovation project that you never got around to finishing, bring it to a scrap metal recycling center and donate the proceeds to your favorite charity.

Angel Power Rule #4

LESS IS MORE

Angel Power Rule #5

TAKE PRIDE IN YOUR WORK

Simplicity is the whole secret of well-being.
— PETER MATTHIESSEN

Have you ever wondered how some people get a lot accomplished in a short period of time?

There are two Rules of Angel Power that will help you accomplish a lot more during your fifteen minutes of mini-miracle working without compromising the end result. The first Angel Power Rule is to make your work as simple as possible, without being simpleminded. The second rule is to take pride in your work: Taking pride can not only have a dramatic impact on your mini-miracle work but, believe it or not, on your life as well. When you use the two rules together, you'll begin to see how a big mini-miracle can be accomplished with ease and simplicity.

Angel Power Rule #4: Less Is More

Envision someone devoting her life to helping others in an impoverished country. This miracle worker wakes up at the crack of dawn every day and gets to sleep late at night. All day, she's caring for the sick and running a school in a makeshift hut, teaching children reading, writing, and arithmetic. In a remote, tiny village, she cooks hundreds of meals for the hungry, ladling out bowl after bowl of nourishing food. Sweat is beading on her face, and she is tired, her muscles are sore, and her back aches. A child cries and she rushes to his side.

Is this your vision of a miracle worker?

When I ask people to envision a miracle worker, they usually paint a picture like the one above, of someone slaving away in a third-world country. It's a pretty common stereotype, and I don't know why. The truth is, not many of us are capable of this kind of selfless devotion, yet all of us can be miracle workers in our own unique way without putting in an endless amount of time.

Because time is one of our most precious commodities, I looked for the secret to achieving amazing results in no time flat. This is what I found: The secret is to reduce the number of steps in a project without harming the end result. You *can* get the maximum amount of work done in the minimum amount of time, I always say. In fact, this is the reason why I'm able to do so much without ever feeling overwhelmed.

My Technique

People often ask me, "How do you do it all?" and "Where do you find the time to have a life?"

The truth is, my work takes, and always has taken, very little of my time, because early on in my life I adopted a technique based on the teachings of Albert Einstein: Make everything as simple as possible, but not simpleminded. Einstein believed you could remove steps in a process, whether it be washing the family pet or launching an international campaign, and still achieve the same, or even better, results in the end. This Angel Power Rule has allowed me to achieve my wildest dreams, but has still afforded me the time to relax and enjoy life. Following Einstein's philosophy—simplification—does not mean you should rush through life; it means being efficient but achieving optimum results.

Today, my time may be more limited, but my enthusiasm and appreciation for life aren't. Even though my own goals have progressed in scope and size as I get older, they are easier to accomplish because I am not idle with inefficiency.

One weekend before Earth Day a few years ago, I volunteered to plant rose bushes in an inner-city botanical garden. Even though the project was arduous, I knew the results would be worth it: Every spring, the rose garden would blossom and bring a sweet-smelling scent to the community. Of course, my continual drive to be as efficient as possible could not escape this project.

I was charged with planting thirty rose bushes. My original instructions were to dig a hole to a specified depth and width, aerate the soil, mix in fertilizer, loosen the root ball of the rose bush, water the hole, place the rose bush in the hole, fill the hole with soil, pat down the dirt with my foot, and mulch. I was to repeat this process thirty times. No matter how quickly I worked on the project, I calculated it would take a few hours to complete. I knew there must be a way to get it done more quickly with the same results.

Scanning the park, I noticed some young people playing basketball. Why not invite them to help out for a few minutes? Having worked with thousands of young people in community-service projects, I know that when given the chance, kids will volunteer their time. This case was no exception.

I gave each young person a job in the planting process. One kid dug the hole while another fertilized and another loosened the root ball, etc. I ran around and pitched in when needed, digging holes and spreading mulch. In about the same time it would have taken me to plant one rose bush, we planted ten. In less than thirty minutes, we finished the project.

The moment couldn't have been better: I had time to stop and smell the roses.

Complicated Mini-Miracles: An Oxymoron

Take a look at your annual platform statement. (If you haven't written one yet, try formulating one now.) What are some simple ways you can further your platform each and every month without taking more time?

Stranded? Check out the story of a gray-haired college student, Mabel Barth, who made a difference for thousands of young people—all because she made everything as simple as possible.

Miracle Worker: Mabel Barth

"I had gone to college with gray hair," says Mabel Barth with a laugh. Mabel, despite my persistent requests, refuses to tell me her age. "One of the things I noticed was how much I needed to sit down and talk to somebody. I wanted to air my feelings and emotions, you know, have a place to talk." Mabel was convinced there were other college students who felt alienated, lonely, and lost, too. She had a simple solution to this problem: Set up a listening post, a table where college students could speak with her on a one-to-one basis about anything that was on their minds. "No advising or counseling here. Just listening."

On April 3, 1979, Mabel started the first listening post. "I was scared to death that day— there were 25,000 students! Why would anyone stop and talk to someone they didn't know?"

But to quote the famous phrase from *Field of Dreams*, "If you build it, they will come." Mabel set up her booth and they came—but only after a bit of bribery. Thinking like a college student, she figured food would be a big draw, so she set out free apples ("I reasoned that apples would work because of their bright colors") and unshelled peanuts at the table. Why unshelled peanuts? "Peanuts in the shell slow down the process of communication," Mabel explains with a laugh. "You know, it takes a long time to open up those shells to get two peanuts. It was an intentional thing...they opened the peanuts, and they opened themselves."

Mabel provided something different from traditional student counseling services: She wasn't judgmental. Students were encouraged to solve their own problems. "We only ask questions, never give advice," says Mabel.

It has been more than twenty years since Mabel set up a table in the student lounge of the Aurora Higher Education Center in Denver and shared snacks and informal conversations with dozens of college students. Today, because of word of mouth, more than 4,000 students a week talk to four hundred trained "grand-parents" at Listening Posts on one hundred campuses across the United States and Canada. "More than two million Listening Post conversations have taken place," adds Mabel.

"I'm not a spectacular person. I had a simple idea of sitting down and listening to someone open up." I asked her what it's like to receive letters from kids who say they now have self-worth, have learned to stop hating people, have rejected drugs and alcohol, and have grown to respect themselves because of Listening Posts. "It's a feeling of awe, it really is."

A simple idea can have an awe-inspiring effect on the world. Mabel believed that college students need a place to talk about their fears, their successes, or to vent their stress. She didn't think big; Mabel didn't need staff members, an administrative budget, or a p.r. budget. All she needed were some snacks, a checkerboard tablecloth, and a hand-painted sign to get started. The fact that her simple program has now spread across the United States and Canada, all by word-of-mouth, is proof that keeping everything as simple as possible can work.

Also, think ahead. It's so much easier to save time when you think ahead instead of trying to save time as you execute the project. Real-time editing is not as efficient. When you plan ahead and remove unnecessary steps, you save time.

The key to creating simple mini-miracles is to plan and think ahead. Learn from mistakes (so you don't duplicate them in the future), and try your very best to prevent waste. There is no reason to devote endless hours to a mini-miracle that could be achieved in less than fifteen minutes. Wouldn't you rather get the same results with much less work?

Making It Simple

Do you remember that *Seinfeld* episode in which Kramer, Jerry Seinfeld's crack-up neighbor, concocts ways to cut steps out of his morning shower routine to save time? As the show progresses, he cuts and peels vegetables in the shower *while* shampooing his hair. "Jerry, I'm loving it in the shower!" He becomes so efficient that he even installs a garbage disposal in the shower drain to prevent it from clogging with vegetable peels.

Of course we don't need to go to this extreme,

but it *is* possible to get the maximum amount of work done in the minimum amount of time. I do not believe that we have to choose between contributing something worthy to humanity—like fighting hunger, poverty, disease, and abuse—and enjoying some hard-earned leisure time. That's why I believe in fifteen-minute miracles. Efficiency allows us to help others while giving us plenty of time to take the family dog for a walk in the woods or pack the bags for a spontaneous weekend trip to the lake.

Here are some ideas to help you simplify your mini-miracle work:

- Don't volunteer set amounts of time. When I was eleven years old, I volunteered at a local animal shelter. My mother would drop me off at 10:00 A.M. every Saturday and pick me up at 5:00 P.M. I assisted the shelter staff cleaning kennels, feeding the animals, and even walking some of the smaller dogs in the field behind the shelter. I was proud that I gave seven hours of my time.

  The problem was that I usually accomplished all of my volunteer activities by twelve o'clock. That left me with more than five hours with nothing to do. There were better things I could have done than sit around the office asking, "Are you sure there is nothing I can do?"

When you contribute your time to an organization, don't necessarily donate specific blocks of time. The key to simplifying your volunteer work is to do it on a project-by-project basis, not by the hands on the clock. Instead, ask the organization ahead of time what needs to be done. Finish your assigned project in a timely, efficient manner and leave when you are finished.

- Follow the demand. I'm perplexed by people who try to raise money for a worthy cause by selling items that they themselves would never purchase. Does that make sense to you? When I was raising money for Oprah's Angel Network, I thought of two items that I would have liked to buy at a discount: gourmet chocolate bars and Gap T-shirts.

I worked with Gap to receive five hundred T-shirts free of charge. I sold them for seven dollars each, $3.50 less than retail. The shirts sold out in only one hour at a popular weekend flea market, and I raised $3,500 for charity with very little work. Because I brought a first-quality product to an eager audience, I was able to create four $875, fifteen-minute mini-miracles in one hour.

You can do the same thing when either raising money for charity or organizing a larger Heaven on Earth activity. If you're organizing a fund-raiser (see page 163), sell things and provide services that people actually need. When organizing a volunteer activity, don't try to bring people to you. Go to where large groups of people already are, like shopping malls, stadiums, high schools, your place of worship, or your workplace, and get them involved on the spot.

- Offer what you know. This is simple enough. Utilize your skills, like an athletic ability or artistic talent, to help others. Catherine Sneed is a shining example of someone who offers a skill familiar to her. With a green thumb and a heart of gold, Catherine is helping to rehabilitate prisoners and show them the way to a better life.

Miracle Worker: Catherine Sneed

"I was working in the jail as a counselor and I was seeing a lot of people returning to jail or dying on the streets after they got out," said Catherine Sneed. "I wondered, why can't they get out and get a job?"

It wasn't until three years later, when Catherine was sitting in a hospital bed, seriously ill with a rare kidney disease, that she came up with an idea to help rehabilitate prisoners. A doctor handed her a copy of *The Grapes of Wrath* and, as Catherine puts it, "in my morphine phase, I thought if I bring people out of jail and have them garden, they can have a connection to the land and heal." When Catherine beat the odds and recovered from her illness, she remembered her idea. Luckily for the hundreds of prisoners who have benefited from Catherine's project, she is a woman of her word.

Catherine convinced the sheriff at the jail to let her create a working garden on an eight-acre plot of land next to the prison. She named it the Garden Project. With a handful of prisoners eager to be outside in the beautiful San Francisco weather, "we cleaned up an abandoned farm that hadn't been used in twenty-five years. We tore down buildings, removed trash and junk—it took a year," Catherine says. "The prisoners did all of the work; they were happy to be outside."

By 1989, more than three hundred prisoners signed up to participate in the project. The small farm produced organic fruits and vegetables, most of them donated to local soup kitchens in the Saint Martin de Poores, California, area. Not only was the garden helping prisoners, it was a valuable source of food for those in need in the community. "It was nice to give this stuff away to really nice people. The prisoners enjoyed giving back, and, in turn, they gained compassion."

But something wasn't right. While prisoners were gaining self-worth, compassion, and mercy, they still had problems finding employment once they were released from prison. Catherine had another idea: Maybe she could turn her garden into a place of employment for ex-prisoners. So she took a year off from work and attended Emerson College in England to study agriculture. Once she got her education, she came back to San Francisco and thought, "I'm a farmer now."

With her new skills, Catherine transformed the garden into a high-output farm that provides employment to more than twelve hundred ex-prisoners. They are paid with money from the sale of produce and they collectively produce more than 120 tons of fresh fruits and vegetables every year. "We're not just making a pretty little garden here— we're saving lives."

The garden has shown many prisoners with drug problems how plants can grow well without chemicals. They see their hard work pay off in the satisfaction of growing fresh fruits and vegetables without using harmful chemical pesticides. For many people, the power of gardening has rehabilitated them and created a positive fresh start in their lives. "I believe in miracles," Catherine says, "but I can't wait for them to happen."

In the beginning, people thought Catherine was flaky; after all, how could a raspberry bush and pumpkin patch help a drug dealer change? Catherine stuck to what she knew, kept the Gardening Project simple, and rehabilitated hundreds of prisoners. She succeeded because she stuck with a skill she knew—gardening— and created an amazing project that helped thousands of people change their lives through the power of rakes, shovels, and seeds.

- Be obvious. Have you ever been in a situation in which you said, "The solution was right in front of me the whole time! It was so obvious!" An effective way to create powerful mini-miracles is to be obvious, think obvious, and do obvious mini-miracles, as Ranya Kelly exemplifies.

Miracle Worker: Ranya Kelly

All of us have done it: We go to the grocery store or alleyway looking for a box to ship something in or pack something in when moving to a new home. So when Ranya Kelly went rummaging through a dumpster for some boxes, she wasn't seeking out a mini-miracle to create. That is, she wasn't until she made a discovery. "I found my box but also discovered there were about five hundred pairs of shoes dumped into the dumpster." Common sense told her to haul the brand-new shoes home. "I filled up my car with shoes and when I got home, my entire living room was filled with them—all types and sizes."

The only problem with the shoes was aesthetic: They all had slashes of yellow paint. Ranya later found out that stores deface their unsold shoes to prevent people from returning them for cash. "I cleaned them up and decided to hand them out to friends and family." But after she gave some away, she still had a few hundred pairs left. "I didn't know what to do with them until a friend suggested I go to a local shelter to donate them," said Ranya.

Ranya delivered the shoes to a Denver, Colorado, homeless shelter on a "really cold day." "There was a woman walking away from me who was pregnant and she had a child next to her. And she had no shoes on. I naively asked why she didn't have shoes and she said they didn't have any shoes that fit her. I had the shoes that fit her." This one moment changed Ranya's life forever. "I grew up in a very caring and loving family and I never really needed anything. But I never realized I was lacking something in my life. It was my ability to show love to someone else that changed my life."

Ranya now had a mission. She discovered

it was the policy of most large retail stores to dump unsold shoes. "This was unbelievable," she says. "I had to stop it." Ranya campaigned several Denver stores and convinced more than fifty of them to stop defacing shoes and instead donate them to her new organization, The Redistribution Center, Inc., a nonprofit organization that collects unwanted items from businesses and matches the collected goods with a human service agency that needs it.

After thirteen years of collecting items for needy people, Ranya's organization has become an intermediary between charities and businesses. "We get phone calls from businesses that have things to donate. We network, find out who needs it, and get the donated goods to the appropriate organization," she explains. Ranya's organization distributes shoes, building supplies, clothing, and food all over the United States and South America. Every week, she accompanies a large tractor-trailer of donated goods to cities across the country and helps to distribute and deliver needed goods to more than seventy-five agencies.

Ranya says, "My inspiration in God and family keeps me going. I would never trade my position. I think there are a lot of people in the world who would want to have their health and family. I've got that, so I consider myself very lucky."

After running her organization for thirteen years, Ranya says, "We have to give back and realize that all people have value."

Obvious solutions are everywhere. Ranya saw a dumpster full of shoes and knew somebody could benefit from it. Waste not, want not. By being observant, you might find something that could benefit someone in need instead of being tossed out in the trash.

There are obvious ways you can help others. Do you have an old computer lying around? Give it to a local school or to a neighborhood kid who desperately needs a computer. Is your health club collecting canned food or children's books for a charity drive this month? Stop at the store and pick up some merchandise and donate it. There are countless obvious mini-miracles out there just waiting to happen.

- Edit, edit, edit, ~~edit.~~ Whenever possible, I write down every single step I need to take to create a mini-miracle or even to finish a household chore. Whether I'm organizing a charitable fund-raiser or just making holiday gifts for my friends and family, I always look for ways to remove steps that are unnecessary without harming the end result.

I write down my goal first. Then I write down every step needed to bring me to that goal, no matter how small. (e.g., #42: Buy postage stamps for invitations; #43: Adhere stamps to invitations; #44: Stuff envelopes with printed invitations; #45: Seal envelopes). You decide how detailed you want each step to be, but the more steps you write down, the easier it will be to edit.

Now for the fun part. I pull out my trusty red marker and eliminate thirty percent of the steps. Some steps that I remove save very little time, like adhering the postage stamps. (I decided to run the envelopes through a postage machine to save five minutes.) But some steps save a lot of time, such as having items shipped directly to an event site instead of to my home. Editing can also save money: Once I have the items shipped directly, I do not need to hire couriers and movers to haul items.

This writing process forces you to predict where time might be wasted. Editing saves you time, keeps you organized, and makes the mini-miracle more enjoyable and less stressful.

You can also apply this idea, as I do, beyond your mini-miracle work. Have thirty errands to do in one day? Planning a special event like a wedding or birthday party? Write down every single step or task you need to accomplish and combine two into one—or just outright eliminate unnecessary work.

Quality Beats Quantity

I am approached every week with projects that I would love to be a part of. But even with the best efficiency techniques, I do not have the time and must turn down many wonderful offers. If I did accept all of these offers, I know what would happen: The quality of my life would suffer.

As astounding as this may sound right now, creating mini-miracles can be addictive. Once you see how easy it is to help others and improve your part of the world, you might be tempted to take on too much. Remember, though, it's better to start small and progress slowly over time. Allow yourself to be challenged and create larger mini-miracles at a pace that is comfortable for you.

After all, one well-thought-out mini-miracle done in an efficient manner is far better than twelve poorly planned mini-miracles that turn into mini-disasters.

Angel Power Rule #5: Take Pride in Your Work

Taking pride in your work does not equate with being stressed out. But I want to hammer home the point that paying attention to details, including so-called insignificant tasks, can have a profound impact not only on your mini-miracles but on your life as well.

For as long as I can remember, I've always taken pride in my work, no matter how small the task. If I made a mistake, though, it never bothered me. Instead, I tried to view the moment as a learning opportunity so I could find a way not to repeat it. The reason I take pride in my work, and you should too, is that I believe every action that I take, even if it seems meaningless, like bringing the recyclables out for recycling, or meaningful, like lecturing before an important audience, has the potential to take me on a different path in my life.

How can taking pride in — of all things — recycling shape my destiny?

The Significance of "Insignificance"

Did you ever accidentally run into a long-lost friend or family member at the post office buying stamps, picking up milk at the supermarket, or walking a different way home? Have you ever known anyone who barely escaped a fire, an accident, or a plane crash? What insignificant thing was that person doing that prevented him from being in that burning building, at that intersection, or on that airplane? Think of "insignificant" acts that ended up having a significant impact on your life. It works the same way with mini-miracles. If a chance meeting at the supermarket can change your life forever, then imagine what can happen if you volunteer to the best of your ability. That personable fund-raising phone call you make could be to a wealthy philanthropist who decides to donate $10,000 on the spot (it's happened to me); changing that burned-out light bulb for an elderly neighbor not later but immediately could prevent her from falling down the stairs—and all because you took pride in your work.

Taking pride in your mini-miracle work is crucial. You have the opportunity to help in ways that are either mediocre or extraordinary. All of us can strive to be extraordinary. And taking extraordinary pride in everything you do will steer your life onto a greater path each and every time.

Path to what? A path to changing the world; a path to a better you; a path to an amazing life lesson. None of us knows what the future holds, but by doing everything to the best of our ability, we can pave the way for the best of everything.

Putting Pride into Action

One of the most important acts I ever did as a child was leading a campaign called Save Hidden Pond.

When I was thirteen years old, I decided to save a sixty-six-acre forest area in Green Hills, Pennsylvania, from being developed into a luxury housing development. My organization, Earth 2000, had only about thirteen members at the time and a budget of $23. Our only other campaign activity was recycling beer cans we collected at the Thriftway supermarket on Saturday mornings. From recycling foul-smelling cans to saving a forest—okay, I'm not even sure where the segue was.

During the campaign, I was constantly learning something new, such as the intricacies of writing a press release or asking donors for money. My critical thinking and public speaking skills strengthened. I took great pride in making sure I did the best job that I could do and, in the process, I learned a great deal.

I researched the history of the land, took careful notes about it, and kept photocopies of everything. I photographed important landmarks, like rare flowers, trees, bridges, and waterways on the property; I didn't know what they were, but I knew my careful documentation might come in handy later. I even had five hundred posters photocopied a second time because of a spelling error.

I worked for more than a year on the campaign. I gave countless media interviews and would talk to anyone about the campaign. If I was approached by a journalist or a confrontational neighbor, I would take pride in making sure I gave information as accurately as I could. I won the support of an environmental attorney, who represented me on a pro-bono basis because she knew how dedicated I was to the project.

After many hearings, many interviews, and many sore throats, I was able to preserve a good portion of the area because the development company was unable to sell lots to the public. Almost everyone in my community agreed the area should be preserved. But the greatest win wasn't the land being preserved, it was learning a valuable skill: I learned how important it is to take pride in everything that I do. My careful documentation of the land, for example, had uncovered a nineteenth-century historical site on the property, which led to the unearthing of historical artifacts. It also got my community talking and thinking about the environment.

Taking pride in my work took me on the road to bigger things. My organization, for example, gained 1,000 new members from the campaign's media exposure. Having more members meant strength in numbers, which led to better campaigning and more funding, which eventually led to the creation of a powerful national organization, which led me to my writing career, which helped me raise large sums of money for worthy causes. All because of taking pride in my work—no matter how small the task.

The Laws of Being Proud

There are three laws of taking pride in your work that I use every day.

#1: I will take pride in my mini-miracle work. For me, creating mini-miracles is one of the most important things that I do. I know it has done so much to make me a better person, to boost my spirits, and to provide hope in a chaotic world. That is why, when you create mini-miracles and want to improve your world and yourself, you must do them with great care and pride.

#2: I will take pride in the workplace. Okay, you're thinking, this rule makes sense, but how does it apply to helping someone in need?

Taking pride in our work isn't something we can just switch on and off. ("I think I'll take pride in my mini-miracle work today, but I'll slack off in writing this proposal.") It's a skill that can only be strengthened through repetition. Your goal is to get to the point where taking pride in your work becomes second nature to you.

It's like learning how to use a computer. The first time, the computer is intimidating and not very user-friendly: Files are deleted, screens freeze, and software doesn't install. But you don't give up. You read the owner's manual, ask friends for help, and call the manufacturer for assistance (even if that means waiting for thirty minutes on hold). After a few weeks, you begin to master the intricacies of using a computer and begin to wonder how you lived without one. If you didn't take pride in learning how to use a computer, it would probably end up catching dust instead of making your life more efficient and productive.

#3: I will take pride in recognizing everyone around me. I go out of my way to thank people for assisting me in a project or in my life. "Thank you for taking the time to speak with me at the conference. I really do appreciate it," or "Thank you for coming out to volunteer at the Schuylkill River cleanup. Your hard work is much appreciated by myself and everyone there." There are dozens, if not hundreds, of people in your life who have contributed or will contribute to your mini-miracle work, helped further your career, or just got you out of a real jam. Take pride in thanking them.

One of the side benefits of working with other mini-miracle workers is that you meet interesting people. I've made many wonderful friendships while volunteering at a river cleanup or making Halloween goody bags for sick children. When someone else selflessly extends himself to others, you know that, as a friend, he will selflessly be there for you.

A Review

Ask yourself: How can I simplify my efforts to help others and make a difference right now? Instead of hand-kneading bread from scratch for the church bake sale, maybe you could ask a neighbor or friend to lend you a bread machine. Let technology work for you, save time, and still achieve the same, if not better, results.

And be sure to take pride in the work that you do.

Taking pride in your work and making things as simple as possible is a balancing act that works.

TEN MINI-MIRACLES
YOU CAN DO TO CHANGE YOUR WORLD

1. Donate an old pair of eyeglasses to the Lions Club. They will be refitted and given to an economically disadvantaged veteran or child with visual disabilities. Call (650) 571-5466 for the drop-off location nearest you.

2. Help a homebound person set up an E-mail account so she can communicate with family and friends around the world. If you're an America Online (AOL) customer, you can set up a free account for her. (AOL customers are allowed up to five screen names per account.) Just set up the software on her computer; then set up her account and password on your computer. When she wants to log on, she signs on as a "guest" and types in her screen name and password.

3. Gather old children's books from the attic and donate them to a public library. Ask your health club to set up a collection box in the lobby and to offer members who bring in at least five books ten percent off next month's dues.

4. Offer to make photocopies of newsletters and fliers for free at your place of work for a scout troop or neighborhood kids' organization.

5. Donate an unwanted bicycle to Pedals for Progress and help provide needed transportation for the working poor. Donated bikes are repaired and sold at a nominal price to people in countries like Nicaragua and Peru. Contact Pedals for Progress, 86 East Main Street, High Bridge, New Jersey, 08829.

6. Give up one impulse item each month, like candy or your daily cappuccino, and give the money you save to charity. (Two dollars a day for one year equals a $730 gift to charity.) Use the money to support the charity of your choice.

7. Ever get the urge to do something homespun, only to end up with partially finished curtains and boxes of sewing products? You can donate sewing notions, fabric, and patterns to benefit sick premature and newborn babies. Newborns in Need makes and gives away blankets for babies born to needy families. Send your materials (monetary donations are appreciated as well) to Newborns in Need, 6078 Lundy Road, Houston, Missouri, 65483-2225, or visit www.newbornsinneed.org.

8. Do you have old videotapes, audio cassettes, or computer disks lying around the house? Instead of tossing them out, recycle them and help fund independent living centers for people who are disabled and homeless. Operation Fast Forward magnetically erases the tapes, repackages them into new products, and sells them. All proceeds benefit the charitable program. Contact Operation Fast Forward, 8012 Remmet Avenue, Canoga Park, California, 91304. (800) 359-4601.

9. Mabel Barth says that "there are millions of people in the world and there are millions of way to help them." She likes to write out a stack of get well cards and drop them off at the hospital. Write some yourself and ask a nurse to give them to patients who have not received cards or flowers.

10. Don't toss out hazardous household waste, like used motor oil or paint, in your regular trash; the toxins could leak into the town's water supply. Contact your local sanitation department to find out when the next hazardous waste pickup is or to find a drop-off location that will dispose of the harmful substances safely.

Angel Power Rule #6

COMMIT ACTS OF
VISUAL PLAGIARISM

*Most of the things worth doing in the world
had been declared impossible before they were done.*

— LOUIS BRANDEIS

The first time my mother visited me in Washington, D.C., her first words to me were, "I hope it rains." She didn't like the way the city smelled or how fast-food containers flew every time a gust of wind picked them off the ground and threw them into the air. But she was expressing in her own way what we all want in our lives: a world that is clean and pleasant-smelling.

It isn't enough to get down on our knees and pray that graffiti, dilapidated buildings, and other visual eyesores will just magically disappear. We must roll up our sleeves and use our hands to create visual mini-miracles.

The Power of Visual Mini-Miracles

Whenever I'm feeling overwhelmed by the world, I turn to the power of mini-miracles. I'll grab a trash bag from my pantry, some heavy-duty work gloves, and pick up debris in my neighborhood. I'll even commit spur-of-the-moment visual mini-miracles: If I'm at the ATM machine, I'll take a few minutes to pick up those little slips of paper strewn all over the ground. I find I can gain a sense of real accomplishment from just a few minutes of hands-on work. And many other caring people across America agree with me.

Hands-on volunteer beautification work, like planting flowers at a hospital, painting the walls of an aging school, or fixing a broken fence at a children's playground, is one of the most popular mini-miracle activities in the United States. It's not hard to see why.

"You see that wall over there? I painted that! It used to be covered with graffiti, but it's nice and clean now," I once overheard a volunteer say. Hands-on work allows us to achieve visible, almost immediate results — instant gratification for a job well done.

And while it may take more than fifteen minutes to create a visual mini-miracle, cleaning up a mess does more than improve the aesthetic beauty of our community. Removing graffiti, for example, also boosts community spirit. Michael Hall, founder of Operation Clean Slate, says that "kids feel like their city is ugly and dirty and graffiti makes them feel bad." Cleaning it up solves several problems at the same time.

Even if painting walls and tilling inner-city gardens isn't part of your mission statement or annual platform, it's important to pitch in anyway. The feeling of dirt crumbling between your fingers, the satisfaction of cleaning a littered beach, or the joy of seeing a child frolic in a playground that was once unsafe reminds us all that our own hands have the power to change the world.

Visual Plagiarism, Visual Plagiarism

I'm always looking for new ways to improve the appearance of my community. One of the techniques I've learned that makes my part of the world as attractive as possible is to the act of committing visual plagiarism.

Visual plagiarism is an idea I came up with a few years ago. Two of my friends were studying the great outdoors as part of an art class field trip. Their assignment was to draw something inspiring from nature: One of my friends picked a picturesque creek overhung by young trees. My other friend, who wasn't as talented, followed her lead and chose the same scene. He also chose identical drawing materials and copied her drawing techniques. He was visually plagiarizing her work. He probably thought, why learn the hard way when someone else has figured it out already? She was a talented artist, after all. He was right. The two pictures, at the end of the day, looked pretty similar. The teacher, however, wasn't amused; my friend received a failing mark for his copycat artwork. But he gave me a good idea: to visually plagiarize mini-miracles.

The idea is simple: If someone else has already figured out the best way to clean up a park or paint a wall, why not use his or her technique? Committing acts of visual plagiarism saves you time and gets the job done in the quickest and most efficient manner. If someone else has already developed the best way to approach a visual mini-miracle, why not copy it?

Okay, isn't plagiarism a bad thing? The dictionary defines plagiarism as "the use of the words or ideas of another as your own." So yes, in an academic or professional environment, it's nothing to be proud of. Copying someone else's work and passing it off as your own original creation isn't just unethical, it's against the law.

On the other hand, it's not against the law to commit an act of visual plagiarism, and nobody will look down at you for doing so; on the contrary, people will think you're smart and efficient. Nobody will be upset if you duplicate his or her mini-miracle work in your hometown. It's flattering.

The ideas in this chapter are the culmination of nine years of visual mini-miracle experience. Many of the ideas are my own, the results of weekend experiments and solutions discovered through trial and error. Many other ideas come from friends and colleagues who have shared their techniques not only for saving time, but also for getting better results.

Taking Stock

Before I commit an act of visual plagiarism, I like to be prepared by having all of the right tools. In my Washington, D.C., home, where space is at a premium, this isn't always possible, and I keep a smaller supply. But even when I'm in rural Pennsylvania with a fully stocked toolshed, I still come up shorthanded occasionally. Some days, I wish I had an extra tarp to catch dripping paint. And other days I wish I had more paint and not so many tarps.

The following is a list of tools you will need to create a well-equipped toolshed. You won't need all of these tools for your mini-miracle work, but whatever you do end up acquiring you can also use for home repairs and improvements.

Essential

- Hammer
- Tape measure
- Nails in different sizes
- Rake
- Pliers
- Screwdrivers, Phillips-head and regular
- Heavy-duty gardening gloves, preferably waterproof
- Large garden shovel
- Paintbrushes and paint tray
- Face mask
- Large canvas tarp
- Recycled 30-gallon plastic trash bags

Nonessential

- Several grades of sandpaper
- Yardstick
- Level
- Hand shovel and trowel
- Pitchfork
- Snow shovel
- Manual hedge cutters (nonelectric)
- Wheelbarrow
- Ladder
- Wire cutters
- Paint sprayer
- Paint scraper

If you don't have all of these items, don't worry. If down the road you need some expensive tools, you don't need to break the bank to purchase them. You can borrow costly tools, like a wheelbarrow or paint sprayer, from your community's parks and recreation department or your county agricultural extension office. Be sure to inform them you need these tools for a community-service project.

Also, you can search yard sales, flea markets,

and the classified section of your local newspaper for great deals on tools.

Now that you've taken inventory of what tools you do and do not have (and you've set some time aside to cruise down the aisles of Home Depot), you're ready to target a site for your first visual mini-miracles.

Getting Started: Finding a Site

Finding a place in your community that could use a little bit of visual enhancement isn't difficult. It's easy to locate places that need help: graffiti-covered walls on your way to work, a boarded-up building near the supermarket, a trash-strewn alleyway near your office.

One of the most important things to remember when choosing a site upon which to commit an act of visual plagiarism is that you must make sure the area can be restored in less than an hour. Any longer and it will become an overwhelming task. Also, make sure it's located on public property.

Why public property? The following story should prevent you from making the same mistake I did.

Earning my driver's license opened up a whole new world to me. Growing up in a mostly rural community with almost no public transportation, I had had my life outside school limited to occasional rides to the shopping mall, courtesy of my mother, and visits to friends who lived within walking distance. Even when I headed Earth 2000 as a teenager, transportation was always an issue that needed to be worked out. It wasn't until I earned my driver's license that my world opened up.

Every morning at 7:45 A.M., I drove to school in my tan 1989 Mitsubishi Sigma along New Holland Road. It was a curvy road that wove around the perimeter of Nolde Forest, a beautiful state park. My older sister Ann had always commented that this was the "fun road to drive on."

One morning, it wasn't so fun: For some reason, traffic was backed up for about half a mile. As I sat in my car staring out the window, waiting for any sign of movement from the cars in front of me, I noticed a large pile of discarded tires sitting among the trees on my left. There were about fifty tires piled on top of each other, covered in mud and spilling into a nearby creek. It was a real eyesore. I decided I would try to organize a cleanup to preserve this small stretch of land when I got to school that day. Twenty minutes later, when I arrived at school, I recruited several friends to volunteer the following Saturday morning.

I purchased heavy-duty work gloves and a tarp to make the task easier to accomplish. I borrowed a sport-utility vehicle that Saturday; we loaded up the car with dirty, foul-smelling tires and made several quick trips to haul the tires to a recycling service in the city, where they were shredded into long strips. After I saw a similar item in an upscale mail-order catalog, I hired a local craftsman, using earmarked funds from Earth 2000, to create durable doormats from the rubber strips. The doormats, I decided, would be sold to raise funds. (To my surprise, the doormats were one of the easiest fund-raisers I ever organized for Earth 2000; once word got out about the indestructible mats, I was able to sell them at four times the actual cost in half the time a product-oriented fund-raiser would normally take.)

The entire cleanup process, from the hauling of the tires to the selling of the doormats, took just a few days to accomplish; it was well worth the effort. The forested area was now pristine; I smiled every time I passed the once-trashed site on my way to school, and my neighbors and friends kept calling to say how much they loved their new doormats.

I enjoyed the activity so much that I wanted to do more, recruit more volunteers, and have more doormats manufactured. My entrepreneurial spirit was coming alive. Not only could I clean up unsightly areas, but I was able to create an in-demand, socially responsible consumer item and raise money for my charity. It was a win-win-win situation, right? Not entirely. Just when I thought I was on top of the world, everything came to a crashing halt.

The land my friends and I so unselfishly cleaned, we were soon to find out, was privately owned. The family that lived on the property, not some careless outsider, had been dumping tires there for years. When they saw the tires being removed, they couldn't have been happier; after all, they had gotten fifty tires removed for free, whereas it would normally have cost them three dollars apiece to dump them legally. Once the area was clear, they filled it up again with used tires in a matter of days. (To this day, I still have no explanation from the family as to why they used so many tires.) When I kindly asked them to utilize the tire recycling service I was using, they began to demand that I pay *them* for moving the tires. This was a case of a mini-miracle becoming a mini-disaster—and one that gave me a major migraine!

As tempting as it may be to help others clean up their property, it isn't your responsibility to take action against their neglect. The best thing you can do for people who create eyesores in your community is to provide information and phone numbers of services that can help *them* clean up their own mess. If they don't take action, you can anonymously contact your local government to see if public nuisance laws can be enforced.

Always pick a public place to create a visual mini-miracle and always obtain permission first from the proper authorities. Contact your local government public works department or police department before beginning your work. When you clean up public property, like a park or playground, and have the support of the local government, they may even offer supplies and services, and the local police may also keep a close eye on your finished mini-miracle project to help keep it pristine.

X Marks the Spot

Consider the following sites for your first acts of visual plagiarism:

- Housing. Without a doubt, if you want to help build decent, affordable housing for families in

need, you can't go wrong with Habitat for
Humanity. To locate a Habitat for Humanity
affiliate in your area, call (800) HABITAT.
Habitat for Humanity will make use of your
home repair and building talent, whether you're
a novice home builder or a Bob Vila clone.

- Schools. Ask your kids or children in your
  neighborhood what needs to be repaired at their
  school. Is the paint in the music room peeling?
  Are some ceiling panels missing? Contact the
  school p.t.a. and volunteer your time to make the
  necessary repairs.

- Parks and playgrounds. A wonderful thing is
  happening in communities across the United
  States. People are joining together and creating
  safe playgrounds from unused public spaces like
  abandoned parking lots. Taking a cue from Habitat
  for Humanity, which uses volunteers to build
  from the ground up, these volunteers construct a
  whole playground from scratch. Sometimes, the
  process is completed in one day, like a barn-raising.
  For links to community organizations building
  magical playgrounds, log on to my Web site,
  www.dannyseo.com. Or, contact your local
  parks and recreation department (the person you

speak with may *be* the parks and recreation department). Ask if they have any planned park improvement days coming up or if there is a special project they can assign to you, like painting a jungle gym at a playground. Be sure to inquire if there are tools you can borrow and if they can provide detailed instructions to help you complete the project successfully.

- Walls. Nothing is a more obvious eyesore than graffiti-covered public spaces. Take a drive or walk around your community and search out graffiti-covered walls, bridges, and doors. Jot down the location and determine whether the area is on public property by contacting the local public works department. If so, obtain permission and gather a few friends to help out by buying some paint, rollers, and a tarp and painting over the unsightly mess.

- Hospitals. While they may not need your help in the e.r., hospitals are a great place to volunteer your outdoor maintenance skills. Contact the volunteer office and offer to plant trees, shrubs, flowers, and grass to help make the exterior as attractive as possible. Sprucing up a hospital or nursing home isn't just landscaping, it can help sick people heal.

Visual Plagiarism #1: Wiping Out Graffiti

Despite its connotations, the word "graffiti" was not coined by gang members or troubled teenagers. The word was originally used by archaeologists to describe drawings and writings found in ancient buildings and monuments in Egypt, Pompeii, and the Roman catacombs. Back then, graffiti was not a form of vandalism, but a way for people to record important or current events of the time.

Today, graffiti has become an obnoxious criminal activity that defaces walls, fences, bus stops, sidewalks, and signposts throughout America. While it's critical that we do something now to clean up the mess, it's also important to go to the root of the problem and prevent future acts of vandalism. One person who has figured out a nearly foolproof way to clean up and prevent graffiti is Michael Hall.

Visual Miracle Worker: Michael Hall

"One day, as I was driving to Los Angeles like I always did, it really struck me. I saw graffiti just about everywhere that I looked," said Michael Hall, a teacher at a juvenile detention center. For someone who "never took a stand for anything," Michael determined he had to do something to solve this problem because he knew it was more than just a visual eyesore: "It was an epidemic."

"Graffiti is bad for the community. It takes seconds to put up, but hours to remove. Kids feel like their city is dirty and ugly. Graffiti scares people, frightens them, and they won't go to a store because they fear gang members might be present. It makes people angry that tax money is going to remove it," he explained.

At the juvenile center, Michael asked his students why they spray painted, or "tagged," walls. "They wanted fame and recognition," Michael said. The more he spoke to young people, the more he realized there was an effective way to prevent and cover graffiti. "A better way to use the kids' time and energy was to do art and go into the community," Michael said. Encouraged by the kids' enthusiasm, Michael created Operation Clean Slate (OCS) and recruited young people, many of whom had "tagged" areas around the city, to clean up graffiti and create beautiful murals in Los Angeles. "Their attention-seeking was destructive and negative, and what I tried to do was put a spin on it into something positive."

More than 5,000 people, from at-risk youth to academic scholars, and 15,000 volunteer hours have gone into painting over graffiti-covered walls and creating murals. Their efforts are working. The owner of an engine parts repair shop in Anaheim, for example, found himself the repeated victim of graffiti. OCS members stepped in, painted a mural of a 1951 Mercury automobile, and a city backdrop. The mural has not been touched by vandals in more than three years now because "the kids painted it and they have friends who know not to touch it." The once graffiti-covered wall also became a conversation piece and source of pride for neighborhood residents to enjoy. "In a lot of cases, murals stop the graffiti problem cold," Michael adds.

All of us can prevent graffiti. There are three simple steps: Identify the problem area, create an immediate solution, and prevent future outbreaks.

Identifying graffiti is a no-brainer task; just make sure the wall or graffiti-covered surface is on public property and obtain permission from the proper authorities before you begin to cover it.

To remove graffiti, all you need is plenty of latex paint (in a neutral color like white or tan), some rollers, paint trays, and a tarp. If you're not sure what you need just ask at the hardware store. Also, many home improvement stores encourage community involvement and may give you free or discounted materials if they're aware of your efforts.

You can also team up with your local p.t.a. to paint a mural on school grounds. (You can order an instructional booklet and video from OCS to take you through the simple process of mural painting.) Michael recommends that you use a high-quality indoor/outdoor water-based acrylic paint, preferably one with a semigloss sheen. While these paints do cost more, it's worth the investment. Be sure to seal the mural with a polyurethane sealant to prolong its life.

You can prevent graffiti by taking a cue from Mother Nature. Plant shrubs and vines at the base of the freshly painted area. The vines will grow onto the wall, and shrubs, especially those with prickly ends, will make it difficult for vandals to spray paint or "tag" the area.

Visual Plagiarism #2: Trees of Life

I try my best every year, no matter how busy I am, to plant or sponsor at least five trees. I believe planting a tree is one of the most productive mini-miracles a person can perform. Not only do trees beautify a neighborhood, but they also provide shade in the hot summer months, help clean our air, provide shelter for wildlife, and sometimes bear fruit for us (and the animals) to enjoy.

While I was doing research for this book, the very first person who came to mind as a visual miracle worker was TreePeople founder Andy Lipkis. Andy is proof that planting trees can change the world.

Visual Miracle Worker: Andy Lipkis

Andy Lipkis wanted to do something meaningful with his life. So, in the summer of 1973, when he read news accounts that smog in the Los Angeles area was killing trees in the San Bernardino Mountains, he leaped into action.

That summer, Andy organized a group of campers to plant smog-tolerant trees "like crazy" to replace a piece of the dying forest. They also swung sledgehammers in an abandoned parking lot, tore up the macadam, fertilized the fresh soil, and planted more trees. In all, they planted more than 8,000 trees that summer. "When we were done, we watched birds, squirrels, grass, and flowers return to what had been a dead parking lot." This experience changed Andy's life so much that he founded TreePeople, with the goal of inspiring people to take personal responsibility for improving their immediate environment through the care and planting of trees.

Over the next few years, Andy's small organization evolved to serve the Los Angeles area through various forestry and environmental education programs. TreePeople teaches children and the community the importance of planting new trees and keeping existing trees healthy. They secure funding from the United States government to pay for the "greening" of the Los Angeles area, run information-rich tree-planting workshops, offer a number of informative books, and teach kids the importance of recycling.

But the heart and soul of TreePeople is the organization's use of volunteers to plant millions of trees. In 1984, before the summer Olympic games, TreePeople coordinated a Million Tree Campaign to plant one million trees across Los Angeles to help the city comply with strict air quality standards. Since trees absorb pollutant gases (nitrogen oxides, ammonia, sulfur dioxide, and ozone), filter particulates out of the air by trapping them on their leaves and bark, provide oxygen, help combat the greenhouse effect, and cool city streets and buildings, Andy knew one million trees could really make a difference. With the power of volunteers, TreePeople met its goal.

Andy points out that planting trees does more than just protect and clean up the environment, increase property values, and help beautify a community. Knowing the power of volunteerism and the cultural and ethnic diversity of Los Angeles, he's seen firsthand how planting trees brings diverse groups of people together. Men and women of all ages, races, economic levels, and professions come together at TreePeople events to improve the quality of life in their neighborhood. Andy says, "I'm happiest volunteering, giving something back, using my powers of persuasion for things that could make the world a better place and relieve the suffering of others."

While many of us may view tree planting as a solely environmental mini-miracle, trees can actually save your city money.

According to the USDA Forest Service, a three-year study found that planting 95,000 trees in the Chicago area would result in a net benefit of $38 million over thirty years by removing harmful pollutants from the air and providing shade during the hot summer months.

If you'd like to plant a tree, but are all thumbs and not a green thumb when it comes to gardening, visit your local nursery, horticultural society, arboretum, or botanical garden for inspiration and advice. Planting trees is easier than you might think.

Also, don't just stick a tree in the ground and pray that it grows. The first two years of a tree's life are the most important and a little care—including water, vertical support, and mulch—will be needed.

If you're planning to plant trees in the city, consider ash, Norway maple, and poplar; they are the best smog-resistant varieties. If you want trees that grow quickly in an urban environment, plant buckthorn, green ash, white ash, various cherry varieties, box elder, or the American elm.

There are different methods, of course, for planting trees in different growing regions. Contact either TreePeople (see resource guide) or your local nursery or horticultural society for directions on planting trees in your neck of the woods.

Visual Plagiarism #3: True Colors

It's a sad fact that many schools in the United States are in terrible shape. Roofs are leaky. Classrooms are overcrowded. Some playgrounds aren't just nonfunctional, they are unsafe.

While educational and children's rights organizations are lobbying Congress for more funding to repair and build new schools and to improve the quality of education, you can make a difference this weekend by upgrading a local school's learning environment with a technique I call Visual Prozac.

Visual Prozac

In recent years, there's been a lot of talk about the psychology of color. Believe it or not, being in rooms that are painted certain colors can make us feel anxious, bored, calm, alert, or relaxed. (I would hate to see what a rainbow-colored room would do to our emotions.)

Color psychology isn't based on some new-agey idea but on accepted truths. According to the Interior Design Institute, we associate colors with objects in the natural world that trigger specific emotions. One color calms us while another may excite. Since most kids spend a good portion of their day in a classroom, painting their classroom certain colors may also help them learn. First, a quick peek into the psychology of color.

- Red: This color is associated with blood or flames from a roaring fire. Restaurants that do not want to encourage lingering use a subtler form of red, like burgundy, to excite their customers; this makes them eat and leave more quickly.

- Yellow: The bright sun and daffodils are good examples of yellow in nature. While yellow makes us feel happy and lively, we tend to tire of it quickly; it becomes oppressive. Pale yellow brings the same positive benefits without the side effects.
- Green reminds us of trees and grass. Light green conjures up images of a breezy spring day. Dark green brings peace of mind. The next time you stroll through a mature pine forest, notice how calm you feel.
- Blue: Restaurants that want customers to linger use blue. (The next time you're at a diner, notice the color of the seats and walls.) Light blue reminds us of the sky and provides a relaxing sensation. (If you don't like to cook, color a block of wood light blue and hang it in the kitchen as modern art; it will calm you.) Blue is the second most powerful color after red.
- White: Fluffy clouds, feathers, and doves conjure images of peace and innocence, right? While one would think a white room would bring peace of mind, it doesn't. The color is too closely associated with hospitals and disposable paper products and so can seem sterile. It also reflects light in the classroom too strongly and can strain the eyes.

- Brown is the color of soil and the color of autumn leaves. It's a neutral color that does not trigger a specific emotion. Another reason why brown rooms aren't all the rage — ever.

If you'd like to improve a school's visual environment, work with the school's p.t.a. and administration to coordinate a Visual Prozac painting weekend, keeping these rules of color in mind. Choose colors that will help a group of children learn by visually solving a problem. For example, if a fourth-grade class tends to be too lively, paint their classroom light blue. If a first-grade class easily gets bored or restless during the day, paint their classroom pale yellow or light green to create a lively, happy environment. It may or may not work, but if even a few students can find the environment more conducive to learning, then it's worth the weekend of time.

Visual Plagiarism #4: Clearing Debris

We've all read news articles about volunteers cleaning up beaches and highways on special cleanup days around the country. It's a great way for a community to bond.

But what if you're alone and discover a great big mess along a highway or in a forest? Don't flag down the next busload of teenagers to help you out, and don't clean up the mess yourself. Join forces with the polluter.

My hometown of Reading, Pennsylvania, hosts an annual weeklong festival called Scenic River Days to celebrate the beauty of the Schuylkill, a 128-mile-long river that flows from Tamaqua, Pennsylvania, through my hometown and empties into the Delaware River. Held along Riverfront Drive in Reading, the festival boasts an impressive selection of native and ethnic foods, live music, non-profit educational booths, and games for the kids.

As the event gained popularity, more vendors were invited, and more people flocked to the event. But the bigger and better it became, the more problems developed. One of those problems, I discovered after all the vendors packed up and left at the end of the festivities, was that trash from the festival was ending up in and along the river. I couldn't believe it.

I saw hundreds of food containers, event flyers, promotional materials, and packed trash bags full of discarded food all over the Schuylkill River banks. I even saw a banner strewn along the riverbank that read, "Celebrate the beauty of the Schuylkill River." The irony was too much. An event that touted itself as a "celebration of the Schuylkill River" was trashing the guest of honor.

While some people would choose to chain themselves to the event organizer's office and demand that the river be cleaned, I saw this as an opportunity to work with the organizer instead. I photographed the trashed areas, collected a few pieces of trash for physical evidence, and met with the organizers. They responded just as I thought they would: They were embarrassed and agreed to help in any way possible.

I visited other festivals around the state to see what they did to control refuse. I watched people purchase food, eat it, and would document how they discarded the waste. Did people bother to recycle? What kinds of trash bins prevented "runaway" trash and what kinds didn't? If someone littered, was he or she fined? I found answers to all of these questions through observation and used my findings to help my hometown's festival solve their trash problem.

Working with the Scenic River Days festival, I asked the city to bring clearly marked recycling bins to the event (they had an unused supply in storage), speed up trash pickup to eliminate the problem of overflowing trash receptacles, ban styrofoam containers, and require the committee to recruit volunteers at the end of the festivities to clean up the riverbanks. I made the event efficient by visually plagiarizing the work of more finely tuned festivals. The next year, the river was spotless.

What I learned most from this experience was to work with the polluters, who were unaware of the problem, to find a solution that wasn't just feasible but effective and simple to do.

Visual Plagiarism #5: This Old House

I have to say that building homes for families in need is truly one of the most gratifying things I've ever done. Nothing has brought me more joy in the last year than my work with Habitat for Humanity. If you haven't done so yet, volunteer with Habitat for Humanity and you'll see why I support this organization so much.

The Habitat for Humanity home I sponsored in Baltimore, Maryland, through Oprah's Angel Network was a dilapidated building in the Better Waverly section of Baltimore. The home was uninhabitable, ruined by fire just weeks before and rotting from excessive water damage over the years. The carpets were soaked, the roof had caved in, and large insects crawled on the floors and walls. Jenny Hope (yes, that really is her last name), the executive director of the local Habitat affiliate that was constructing the home, said my $30,000 gift would be used to renovate the house. I felt it couldn't be done for that amount of money.

On the official ground-breaking day, I was surrounded by *Oprah* viewers who volunteered to help build the home; even though there was a large turnout of volunteers, I felt skeptical that we could succeed. It certainly didn't help my confidence to hear the volunteers around me saying, "I've never done anything like this before, either!" Could a group of novice home builders who probably own VCRs that still flash "12:00...12:00...12:00" build a home? I would have taken the Vegas odds that the house would never be built.

Even though I felt skeptical, I saw that the volunteers did have plenty of energy and enthusiasm; that's the kind of energy Dale, the construction manager, desired in his workforce. Each day Dale taught a crash course in home repairs, whether it was tearing down drywall or installing a kitchen sink. The volunteers, I discovered, learned skills quickly with his direct and down-to-earth instructions. To my surprise, I saw these same volunteers tear down walls and rip up floorboards with an amazing amount of energy and gusto. (Personally, I think one woman was working out some issues with each swing of the sledgehammer.)

Just three months later, the home was unrecognizable. The floors were covered with a light blue wall-to-wall carpet. The energy-efficient windows, front and back porches, and tidy backyard were highlights of the new home. It was amazing. Jenny had been right.

The core of Habitat for Humanity is the volunteer. In my opinion, there is no other organization in the world that so effectively utilizes the skills, energy, and enthusiasm of volunteers. Volunteers offer an hour, a day, a week, or a month to build homes with future home owners; they provide virtually all of the house-building labor. The new homes provided for families aren't handouts; they're a hand up. Families who receive homes are required to purchase them at cost, financed with interest-free loans.

But the new homes go beyond just providing housing for a family. Habitat for Humanity believes that by freeing families from the unending struggles that accompany inadequate shelter, these homes open the door to increased self-esteem and self-reliance. And, in turn, families can devote more attention to job opportunities, education, and health. The cycle of poverty is broken, their children learn real-life survival skills, and the neighborhoods change for the better. And Habitat has even helped change the world a little bit at a time, with Protestants and Catholics in Northern Ireland working side by side on building homes, "united by the theology of the hammer."

When I began writing this book, I decided not to single out one specific charity to support. But the more I got involved with Habitat for Humanity, the more my belief in the program strengthened. There are more than 300,000 people worldwide who have received housing through the organization, but there are millions more still living in substandard conditions, and thus I undertand the urgency of the organization's mission. That's why a portion of the proceeds from this book is benefiting this organization and why I urge you to get involved with them.

Visual Plagiarism #6:
Creating an Eden Alternative

What comes to mind when you think of a hospital or nursing home? Sterile? Unimaginative? Dull? When Dr. William Thomas thinks of a hospital or nursing home, the word "paradise" comes to mind.

Miracle Worker: Dr. William Thomas

Dr. William Thomas discovered a medical breakthrough a few years ago that reduced his patients' infections and need for medication by as much as fifty percent and decreased their death rate by a whopping twenty-five percent. What amazing miracle drug did Dr. Thomas develop? Well, it's not a groundbreaking pharmaceutical substance. It's a living garden at a nursing home.

Dr. Thomas is the medical director of an upstate New York nursing home. Believing that an isolated environment with little stimulation or interaction is bad for patients, Dr. Thomas wanted to liven up the joint. "Most nursing homes make a desert look great," he says. "What they offer is loneliness, helplessness, and boredom." So he created a home that broke all the rules: He brought in animals and started to grow a garden.

Dr. Thomas turned lawns into tilled patches where residents could grow their own vegetables. He filled their rooms with plants and encouraged them to take care of animals in their rooms as well. Throughout the nursing home were parakeets, dogs, and cats—a total of 137 animals. Outside were chicken coops and even a rabbit hutch. Many of the residents were given daily duties to care for the animals and plants.

The results of this anti–nursing home experiment are amazing: Patients are rejuvenated, happy, and develop self-worth by having the responsibility of taking care of plants and animals. "There's no way I as a physician could get results like that, even if I saw every patient every day," says Dr. Thomas. "I believe the Eden Alternative is a powerful tool for improving the quality of life for people who live in long-term care facilities."

Susan Chernak McElroy, author of *Animals as Teachers & Healers*, agrees; she believes animals have the power to heal us. From personal experience, Susan credits her triumph over terminal illness to the love of her dog, Keesha. She writes: "In their innocence and wisdom, in their connection to the Earth and its most ancient rhythms, animals show us a way back to a home they have never left." And that's how Dr. Thomas's gardens work to help the sick and dying.

The impact of his work has not gone unnoticed by other medical institutions. Dr. Thomas's Eden Alternative idea spread to hundreds of other nursing homes that adopted his philosophy. Today, once unengaging environments are lively, nurturing, happy places where friendly dogs, colorful zinnias, and rows of corn thrive side by side with patients. "We must teach ourselves to see long-term care facilities as habitats for human beings rather than institutions for the frail and elderly. We must learn what Mother Nature has to teach us about the creation of vibrant, vigorous habitats."

You don't have to go to the extraordinary lengths Dr. Thomas did to improve his nursing home, but you can perform a smaller version of his miracle work.

In the spring, you can either grow or purchase small houseplants at the nursery to give to nearby nursing home residents. Be sure to include instructions on how much light and water the plant will need to thrive. You can also bring your dog (if he's well disciplined) to meet the residents; just be sure to give him a bath before he heads off to the home, make sure he's housebroken, and obtain persmission from the home. You can also get permission from the administration to create an easy-to-grow lima bean patch, a salad garden, or sunflower field in the backyard of the nursing home; encourage the residents to help out by watering and weeding the mini–"Garden of Eating."

Plagiarizing from Other Sources

You don't have to limit your acts of visual plagiarism to these ideas. You can find ideas from a variety of sources.

- Magazines: Niche publications specializing in gardening, home decorating, and home repair offer timesaving tips that can be applied to your mini-miracle work. Recently, I learned how to decorate a room on a dime, repair a wooden fence, plant shrubs and trees, and wire lighting fixtures from articles in *Garden Design, This Old House,* and *House & Garden.* I can not only apply these skills to my home but to my visual mini-miracles as well.

- Television: News programs like *Dateline NBC, 60 Minutes, 48 Hours,* and shows on CNN profile miracle workers all the time. The next time you see a profile story, don't just sit back and watch. Grab a piece of paper and a pen, and take notes as if you were attending a class. Find an idea you like and visually plagiarize it.

- Manufacturers: A few years ago, the Salem Paint Company of Salem, Oregon, started to collect old cans of latex paint. The paint was collected free of charge from the town's residents, tested for contamination, remixed, and given to volunteers who used it to paint over graffiti. The company also provided step-by-step instructions for properly painting over a surface, saving time for the good-hearted citizens who got involved.

Companies are always looking for ways to serve the community in which they do business. They will often provide free supplies and suggest timesaving techniques to make sure your mini-miracle goes smoothly.

It's easy to improve the visual quality of our neighborhoods. By doing something as simple as picking up an aluminum can off the ground instead of just walking right by it, or buying a tray of ivy to plant at the base of a freshly painted wall, we can all make a difference.

Ten Mini-Miracles You Can Do to Change Your World

1. Buy organic produce from inner-city working gardens that provide employment to previously homeless people. In the city of Houston, Texas, for example, Urban Harvest runs more than forty-seven inner-city gardens that produce tens

of thousands of pounds of fresh produce every year. The produce is sold to the public and given to local soup kitchens and senior centers. Log on to Microsoft Network's www.sidewalk.com to find an inner-city working garden near you.

2. Clear trash, repair a fence, or remove weeds from a historic or neglected cemetery. Be sure to obtain permission first from the historical society or local government agency that controls the property.

3. If your community is raising money to build a playground, become a sponsor. Many organizations sell "bricks" for a set amount. An actual brick will be laid in the playground with your name, or your special message, engraved on it for future generations to see and play around.

4. Lean branches in uncovered basement window wells so creatures like chipmunks and rabbits who fall into them can climb out.

5. Call the local fire company and ask if they need volunteers to work on the grounds or in the firehouse. Some chores they might need help with include painting walls or pulling weeds.

6. Plant vines at the bottom of a freshly painted wall; the vines will grow onto the wall and prevent graffiti.

7. Contact the city public works department immediately if you notice a streetlight that's burned out.

8. If you spot an injured animal, whether it be a dog or wild bird, contact the local humane society or wildlife rehabilitation center and they'll send a trained person out to help. Keep these phone numbers handy by your telephone and in your automobile if you have a cellular telephone.

9. Prevent fire from ravaging your neighborhood and taking someone's life. Install a smoke alarm in the home of an elderly neighbor; be sure to follow up every few months to replace the battery.

10. Buy a trash can with a tight-fitting lid that cannot be easily knocked off by a strong gust of wind or a wild animal. Trash that is not properly stored can scatter throughout the neighborhood, creating a real eyesore.

Angel Power Rule #7

DOUBLE YOUR PLEASURE, DOUBLE YOUR FUNDS

We make a living by what we get.
We make a life by what we give.

— WINSTON CHURCHILL

When I was eight years old, I began to steal the Publishers Clearing House sweepstakes entry kit from my parents' mail. I would hide the envelope declaring "Dr. J. Seo: You may already be a winner" under the living room couch, and, when nobody was paying attention to me, would fill out the entry forms. I devoted a great deal of time to being accurate on the forms (perhaps too much), even debating at great length which color Jaguar I'd pick if I won the "early bird" prize. Every year I thought, "Yes, this year I will win."

If I had won the grand prize of one million dollars, I wouldn't have bought a fancy house or embarked on an exotic vacation; I would have given my father the Jaguar and donated the money to charity.

Yes, I realize I was only a child and didn't fully understand the value of money (all I knew was that a big coin and little silver coin got me a candy bar), but I did understand that money could help people. And I knew one million dollars could help a lot of people.

Of course, I—or Dr. J. Seo—never won. It was my very first in a series of failed fund-raising attempts. (That isn't to say I never won a contest. When I was ten years old, I entered my mother in a Weis supermarket contest to win a Ford truck. Since she had no idea I had entered her, she thought it was a scam artist on the phone when the contest organizers called her one morning to give her the good news that she won. She turned down the prize, probably thinking, "I watch *20/20;* I know about these scams." When I returned from school that day, I couldn't believe she'd done that. Lesson learned: Develop better communication skills with parents.)

Anyway, the reason I wanted to give one million dollars to charity is directly linked to a lesson I learned at church. During the holiday season at Robeson Lutheran Church, the congregation was asked to bring household items, like canned food and shampoo, to be given to families in need in our community. I went with my mother to the service one morning when I was seven years old and deposited our gifts—a couple of boxes of facial tissue—into the holiday collection box. (The evening before, I spent a whole hour gift-wrapping the tissue boxes. I look back at that chore today and think, Why would anyone gift-wrap boxes of Kleenex?) It felt good to give. It is that same emotional feedback—feeling good about myself through giving—that drives me to be generous today. I found joy in it.

There's an old saying that money can't buy love. I disagree. Money, when used to create mini-miracles, can buy love: a new roof for a family in need, nourishing food for a hungry child, or repairs to a broken playground. You may find this unbelievable right now, but the more money you give or raise, the more mini-miracles will be created and the better you will feel about yourself. It's the easiest path to self-improvement and happiness.

How Generous Are You?

Do you consider yourself a generous person? Maybe you give money to PBS during their pledge week, or you responded to a fund-raising appeal you received in the mail—in 1993. Okay, maybe you don't contribute large amounts of money, but you might think, "It's not how much you give, but that you give at all." I disagree. The truth is that it does matter how much you give. In my opinion you should give at least five percent of your annual income before taxes to a worthy cause.

Now that you've had a moment to calculate that amount and to roll your eyes in disbelief, you'll be surprised to learn that you probably already give quite a bit of your annual income to charity.

How much do you really give each year? Try the following exercise:

1. Pull out your checkbook or tax returns from last year and write down how much you gave in straightforward tax-deductible contributions, like a $50 check made out to the United Way. Write the total amount here: $ _____ .

2. Go into your kitchen cabinets, bathroom, garage, and desk and collect every single item that you purchased that benefits a charitable cause, like Girl Scout cookies, Sierra Club calendars, and Newman's Own food products. Add up the retail prices (if you have to estimate, it's okay), deduct eighty-five percent of the amount, and write it here: $ _____ . (Generally, about fifteen percent of your purchase price actually benefits a charity.)

3. Did you donate a used car, computer, clothing, furniture, housewares, or any other consumer items to charities like Goodwill Industries or the Salvation Army? If so, you should have received a receipt (for tax purposes) for the items' estimated retail value. Add up the total amount of the receipts for last year and deduct fifty percent; write that amount here: $ _____ . (You need to deduct fifty percent to reflect the fact it wasn't a monetary donation; charities do benefit from gifts of durable goods, but they need to pay overhead costs as well.)

4. Did you donate your frequent-flier miles to a charitable cause? Give yourself $.40 for each mile donated. For example, if you donated 1,000 miles, then you would write $400. Write the amount here: $ _____ .

5. Figure out how many times you dropped pocket change into those collection boxes you see at restaurants and retail stores. How much money do you put in each time? Twenty cents? Fifty cents? A dollar? Multiply that amount by forty-eight (people give, on average, about four times a month) and write that amount here: $ _____ . (Incidentally, those collection boxes are usually scams and you should discontinue giving to charity that way if you have in the past. See page 179 for more information.)

6. When you're shopping, do you throw spare change into the mall's fountain? (Most malls donate these coins to charity.) How much money do you put in each time and how often do you practice "aquatic philanthropy"? Multiply the amount of money you "toss" each time by the total number of times you give per year (e.g., $.50 x 36 = $18). Write the amount here: $ _____ .

7. Did you attend charity fund-raisers last year, like an awards banquet or art show? Write down the total amount you spent on tickets, food, and items you purchased at the fund-raiser and subtract sixty percent of that amount. (You need to subtract sixty percent because the charity needs to cover its

costs; on average, they earn a profit on about forty percent of your special-events purchases.) Write the resulting amount here: $ _____ .

8. Did I forget anything? Write down any other additional monetary contributions you made to charity: $ _____ .

Now add everything up and complete the following:

A. What is your annual income, including income earned from investments and other sources, before taxes? $ _____ .

B. Multiply that amount by .05 and write your answer here: $ _____ .

C. Write your total charitable giving (from items 1 through 8) here: $ _____ .

D. Subtract line B from line C and write your answer here: $ _____ .

So, are you surprised at how much or how little money you give each year? For most of you, throwing coins into a water fountain and eating Girl Scout cookies probably never counted as giving, but it matters nevertheless.

In 1997, more than $143.5 billion was donated to charitable causes. Good and bad news. While that is a lot of money, it only represents about two percent of every American's annual income. If everyone increased his or her giving to just five percent, more than $350 billion could be given to charitable causes.

I think five percent is a fair amount. I figure if we're willing to pay sales tax at the register (in most states, it's more than five percent) without putting up a fight, then five percent of our annual income is an amount all of us can manage to give to charity.

Four Methods of Personal Giving

Consider the four most popular ways to give:

1. A simple donation is made any time you send a check to a charity or respond to a fund-raising appeal from a nonprofit organization. Most of the time, your donation is tax deductible if the charity is an IRS-recognized, tax-exempt 501(c)(3) registered corporation.

2. Whenever you donate goods, like canned food, clothing, furniture, computers, a used automobile,

or any household item, to a charitable organization that either collects and distributes the items to the needy or sells the donated items to support their work, you are giving. Because most of us are relieved to get rid of unwanted clothing or a junked car in the driveway, it's also not the most generous way to give.

Whenever you purchase a cup of coffee at a high school football game, a box of cookies from the Girl Scouts, or wrapping paper from a church holiday fund-raiser, you are supporting a worthy cause, too.

3. There are several ways money can be automatically deducted from your paycheck or charged to your credit card and given to a charity:

- Credit: Many charitable organizations offer the option of having a predetermined donation charged to your credit card each month. You can even charge you donation over the Internet; just make sure you provide the information on a secure form. The advantage of giving with a credit card is that if you participate in an earned points program, like frequent-flier miles or monetary rebates, you actually earn premiums by giving.

- Combined Federal Campaign (CFC): Federal employees, both civilian and military, have the option of supporting a philanthropic cause through this employee-focused, cost-efficient campaign. This is the only approved charitable solicitation campaign offered by the federal government.

  An estimated forty-one percent of all federal employees participate by selecting a charity from a list of eligible recipients and designating where they would like their payroll deductions to go. The program operates in more than 470 localities throughout the United States, Puerto Rico, the Virgin Islands, and in overseas military bases.

  Approximately $190 million is raised every year for charitable causes through the CFC. The United Way Charities is overwhelmingly the most popular choice, with more than $50 million in pledges received every year through the CFC.

- Workplace giving: If you're not a federal employee, you can still participate in workplace giving programs. While you may not have the luxury of choosing from a directory of hundreds of charities, you can still support a local or national organization by having a predetermined amount deducted from your paycheck.

- Part-time deduction: When I worked at the Gap in Reading, Pennsylvania, as a teenager, the manager asked me if I wanted to have an amount deducted from my paycheck every week to benefit the United Way. I gave twenty-five cents.

A lot of consumer-oriented retail outlets encourage their employees, both part-time and full-time, to give through programs like this. And those quarter donations add up. Let's assume The Gap has 10,000 employees and 5,000 agree to give a quarter every two weeks. In just one year, those quarter contributions total $30,000. Add another nickel to the monthly donation, and the amount balloons up to $36,000, more than enough to build a Habitat for Humanity house or fund a yearlong program for inner-city kids.

4. Accidental donation is made by throwing spare pocket change into the shopping mall fountain or dropping a dollar bill or two into a Salvation Army holiday bucket. For most of us, this isn't so much a way of giving as a convenient way to unload some heavy pocket change.

And, of course, responding to a beggar on the street with a handful of change or a dollar bill is charity, too.

The Joy of Giving

For me, giving is really a selfish thing to do; in less than two minutes, my mood is improved and my daily mini-miracle is accomplished. It's easy and brings fulfillment to my life.

There are many reasons people give to charitable causes. What moves you to be generous?

- Empathy: A natural disaster in Florida leaves hundreds of families homeless. A local child needs money for a bone-marrow transplant. These are just two examples of tragic events that can move us to give. Empathy is the heart and soul of giving. It's gratifying to see how our $20 check can help a family rebuild their lives or a child receive the lifesaving surgery she so desperately needs.
- Joy: When people are financially and emotionally secure, they give to charity as a thankful gesture to the "higher powers" for bringing them to this good point in their lives. Whenever we are happy, we want to share our joy; giving to charity is one way to share our abundance.

- Honor: When a relative dies, grieving family members often request that money that would have been spent on flowers and cards be given to a charitable organization supported by the late family member.

- Economics: When I was running Earth 2000, I remember getting a flood of donations around December 20 each year. Why? Had a vision appeared in the public's morning coffee urging them to "give money to Earth 2000...*now!*"? Perhaps. But I think the practical explanation for why people give near the end of the year is financial. Since they can deduct the amount they contribute from their taxable income, people give to charity because it saves them money. Sometimes a whole lot of money. Often, a donation can move taxpayers from a high tax bracket to a lower tax bracket. A lot of people are moved to give, sometimes very generously, to get a tax deduction before the end of the calendar year.

- A vision: While some people dream of one day living in a mansion, surrounded by expensive artwork, and of owning luxury automobiles, many people dream of spending their time helping others and improving their communities. One of those dreamers is Olga Bloom.

Miracle Worker: Olga Bloom

Olga Bloom had a dream. A retired concert violinist, Olga had dreamed about creating a place where musicians would have total creative freedom, a place where they could rehearse, a place where concerts could be played. Then, in 1977, Olga made an unlikely move: She and her husband mortgaged their home and purchased an old coffee barge, a 102-footlong boat once used by the Erie Lackawanna Railroad to haul coffee, and began to renovate it into a nonprofit floating concert hall.

Even though Olga and her husband knew nothing about construction or even how to finance such a huge project, she wasn't worried. This was her dream and she was fulfilling a lifelong vision. "It was like the reverse of Mephisto. I sold my soul to God and then everything I needed came just when I needed it."

Fortunately for the hundreds of talented musicians who rehearse and perform in the concert hall today, Olga is a woman who believes in her project. When her husband died suddenly, "the dream could have died with him." But instead of giving up, Olga towed the barge to the Brooklyn waterfront, rented out her home, lived off her Social Security checks, and began to renovate the boat all by herself. Over the next two years, she converted the boat into a beautiful wood-paneled concert hall with glass walls behind the stage that give panoramic views of the East River and lower Manhattan skyline.

Aptly named Bargemusic, Olga's vision not only provides an acoustically perfect setting for musicians but has become a beloved attraction for locals and tourists. With more than 12,000 people attending concerts on the barge every year, the boat has proved to be an economic boon to the neighborhood. And to help pay for the barge's operation expenses, Olga rents it out for weddings, special events, and bar mitzvahs.

Bargemusic presents concerts every Thursday evening and Sunday afternoon, fifty-two weeks a year. Even today, after more than twenty years of service to keep Bargemusic afloat (no pun intended), Olga still works round-the-clock.

What keeps her going? "I think virtue is the most exciting way to go. Unquestionably."

Think about the last five times you gave to charity and how good it felt to give. You may have written a check, dropped spare change into the Salvation Army buckets during the holiday season, or bought candy from a child for a school fund-raiser. What emotional reason led you to give? Once you've figured it out, think of the energy you felt from giving. Now harness that energy. That's the energy you should draw on each time you think of giving.

Create an Annual Giving Platform

Another platform?

If I gave you a thousand dollars to give away to a worthy cause, would you divide it up and give it to several charities, or donate all of it to one organization? Don't put all your eggs in one basket, right? However, if you have the opportunity, I encourage you to give generously in one lump sum to just one charity per year.

When I raised $30,000 in January of 1998 to build a Habitat for Humanity house, I saw firsthand how a large gift can make a difference: It built a beautiful house where an ugly building used to be.

Thirty thousand dollars is a lot of money, but hear me out.

Let's assume you give, on average, $2,000 a year to charity. If you give to twenty, ten, or even five different charities throughout the year, the impact isn't as dramatic; it doesn't get the maximum amount done. If you give the $2,000 donation to one charitable organization, and in one lump sum, not only can it significantly advance a campaign or charitable project but you brighten the lives of some of the hardest working people around: a charity's full-time miracle workers.

Staff members at charitable organizations don't work there for the money or perks; they do it because they believe in the cause. I was a volunteer CEO of my own charitable organization, and every time somebody sent a significant contribution, it was like a ray of light: We were thrilled that someone believed in our work. It reenergized us to work even harder. Wouldn't you feel great if you could not only significantly support a worthy cause but also bring joy to those working to create miracles? In essence, you can create many mini-miracles with this one simple act.

If you can't give one lump-sum payment each year, I urge you to create an annual giving platform to support one charitable organization every year. If you send a monthly $20, $50, or $100 check, especially to a small charity where people, and not computers, open the mail, your monthly check will also serve as a regular pat on the back for the charity.

Eight Ways to Double Your Gift... in No Time Flat

If you think that you give all that you can possibly give, then this section will open up your eyes and, ahem, your wallet. No matter who you are and no matter how much you give, you can increase the amount you donate without having to actually give more of your own money. No, I'm not talking about counterfeiting; I've got seven easier and *legal* ways to increase your personal gifts to charity. And one of the easiest ways to double, triple, or even quadruple your gifts to charity is to team up with your employer.

While it would be nice to believe that corporations support nonprofit organizations out of the goodness of the board of directors' hearts, it would be naive to think so.

The fact is, most corporations give out of an odd mix of self-interest and altruistic intentions. The dodgier question is where the former ends and the latter begins. It's important to remember that corporations aren't in the business of giving away profits; they're in the business of making money, and fulfilling their obligations to customers, stockholders, and—most important—to you, their employees.

According to the Foundation Center, there are two main reasons why corporations support nonprofit organizations: (1) to influence legislators and other opinion makers, and (2) to improve the quality of life in the geographic locales in which they operate so the community becomes a healthier place to live and do business.

Most public relations departments and corporate CEOs see publicity potential in awarding grants to charities and often expect a concrete reward in return for their generosity. Giving to worthy causes is also good for the company's image in the media and that, in turn, boosts employee morale. It projects good citizenship while generating profits.

If you're an employee of either a major conglomerate or a small community-based organizaton, you have the influence and power to determine where thousands or even millions of dollars are contributed based on your beliefs.

Some effective ways to significantly increase your gifts to charity include:

Matching Gifts

Major corporations are some of the biggest cheerleaders when it comes to encouraging their employees to give to charity. So much so, that many offer programs that will match, dollar-for-dollar, an employee's contribution to a tax-exempt, 501(c)(3) charitable organization. Ask your human resources director if your company has such a program in place; if not, suggest that they start one.

Foundation Requests

What do Levi Strauss & Company, Gap, AT&T, Ben & Jerry's, and Aveda have in common? Besides being big-name companies, they run their own charitable foundations that support a number of worthy causes.

If you work for a big company like the ones listed above, you can request that the corporate foundation support a charity you give to. Being an employee of the company gives you some say in which charities get supported and which do not.

Even part-time employees can request gifts. When I worked part-time at Eddie Bauer in high school, I read the employee manual and discovered that each store was authorized to give $1,000 to a local charity. Since no one else had bothered to read the manual or fill out the request form, I secured the money to support my charity in the less than fifteen minutes it took to discover the program.

Contractual Clauses

This is my favorite idea. When professional football player John Hannah received a $30,000 signing bonus from the New England Patriots, did he buy himself a brand-new car? Nope, he gave the money to his friend John Croyle to start a ranch for abused and abandoned boys in Glencoe, Alabama.

While you may not have the luxury of receiving a handsome signing bonus, you can use your career to raise money. In a favorable job market, when employers are fighting to find skilled workers for their company, you can add a clause to your contract requiring a company to give a certain amount to a charity of your choice. Even if you're already employed, you can at least ask to renegotiate your contract for the purpose of adding such a clause. And if you're worried about coming across as greedy, don't; nobody will accuse you of being greedy when you are trying to raise money for a charity.

Anonymous Matching Gifts

Have you ever watched a PBS pledge drive when it is announced that if you call at a specific moment, an anonymous donor will match your gift; that is, if PBS raises one million dollars in pledges, then it doubles to two million because of the anonymous donor? I encourage you to give all that you can possibly give when your pledge will be matched.

Paid Volunteers

A contradiction in terms? Not really. Many corporations encourage their employees not only to give money to charity but also to volunteer their time, energy, and talents to the organization of their choice.

US West, for example, runs the Employee Volunteer Grants Program. Full-time employees of US West can track their volunteer time after six months of employment with the company. For each hour of volunteerism, the employee is paid an hourly rate of $6, with a maximum of 100 hours matched per year. That's $600.

If you already volunteer with an organization, then it makes sense to fill out the simple paperwork to get paid for it. You can even donate your "salary" to the charity you volunteer for, too. Not only do you give more financially to that charity, you can deduct your "salary" from your taxable income.

Don't Burn Money

We've all burned money. Burned money involves purchases of items we didn't need, possibly have never used, and that are now just filling up space in our homes. Aren't there better things to do with money than buying a kitchen gizmo that will end up languishing in its original box? When we waste money, we waste an opportunity to make a difference. Here are five signs that you burn money:

—Your garage no longer houses your car; it's filled from front to back with boxes of "things."

—You buy a storage box for the purpose of putting "stuff" into it.

—You cannot remember what your last five purchases were.

—The price tags still hang on clothing purchases you made more than six months ago.

—Your kitchen cabinets are packed with food, yet you still think there is nothing to eat and make a trip to the supermarket.

The next time you go shopping, before you purchase an item, just ask yourself if buying that new item will make your life more meaningful and easier. If so, go ahead and splurge. If not, follow the technique my good friend Ameri taught me: Pick up the item that you desire but don't really need and carry it around the store for a few minutes. Sooner or later, the urge to splurge will move on.

In Lieu of Gifts

If you're expecting friends or family to give you gifts for your birthday, you can ask them to instead make a contribution to the charity of *their* choice. Why their choice? People do not like being told what they can and cannot give; it defeats the purpose of being generous. When you give them the choice of what charity gets supported, you allow them to keep control over their acts of giving and their acts of generosity as well.

Free Service

I give about thirty lectures a year at colleges, corporate retreats, and conferences. Now and then, I will donate my honorarium to a worthy cause; I so much enjoy giving lectures, meeting interesting people, and traveling to new places that it hardly seems right to be paid.

If you're self-employed, consider donating the fee you would receive from one project to a charitable cause. As you would normally, ask to be paid for your service and have the check written out to you. For tax reasons, you should write out a check from your checking account in the exact amount of your fee to the charity of your choice. That way, you can deduct your contribution from your taxable income.

If you're not self-employed, consider donating part of your commission or bonus from one week to charity.

Spying on Yourself

Now that you've learned how to double your personal gifts to charity, and how sometimes it's just a matter of filling out a form or reading the employee manual, you can put your energy where it's needed most: fund-raising.

So, why do you need to raise funds if you and your company can give thousands of dollars to charity? First of all, if you're self-employed (as I am), this is a great way to raise large sums of money to assist a charity. Second, fund-raising is easy.

If you're like most people, you do not enjoy fund-raising. I did an informal poll of my friends and asked them what came to mind when I said the word "fund-raising": "boring," "uninteresting," and "intrusive" topped the list and I was not surprised.

At a very young age, I found myself in the odd position of being chief fund-raiser for my organization. I dreaded fund-raising; it was always difficult, took lots of time, and the results were very unpredictable.

The year that I adopted the philosophy "get the maximum amount done in the minumum amount of time," I analyzed my fund-raising tactics. Why was I baking hundreds of cookies when I could just ask a bakery for an unsold batch? Why wasn't I using the skills of our members? Why didn't I ask wealthy corporate CEOs for money?

I viewed my fund-raising efforts from the outside and saw all the mistakes I was making. I discovered I was not learning from my mistakes. By spying on myself, my fund-raising improved and has since become one of my favorite activities.

Thirty Thousand Dollars in Thirty Days

Now I want you to meet a fella who raised
$30,000 in thirty days all by himself
to pay for our Oprah angel house in Baltimore.
This is Danny Seo... And he says it is not hard
to raise money and change the world.

—OPRAH WINFREY, JANUARY 22, 1998

It really isn't hard to do.

As you know by now, the idea for this book came from my appearance on *Oprah* in January of 1998 to discuss how I was able to raise $30,000 in less than thirty days. What many of you don't know is how I developed a fund-raising plan that not only brought me to my $30,000 goal but used none of my own money up front, took very little time to do each day (about an hour a day for a month), and lived up to my "get the maximum amount done in the minimum amount of time" philosophy. The secret? I spied on myself.

These are the four questions that I asked myself before I began fund-raising:

1. What consumer products would I like to buy at a discount? I thought that Gap T-shirts (which seem to be the only Gap items never marked down) and expensive Belgian chocolate would be desirable products.

2. How could I get cash quickly? I remembered that in my neighborhood, there was an upscale clothing store that sold used designer clothing on a consignment basis. Also, a CD store and bookstore purchased used CDs and books from the public for cash up front.

3. Who would I need to contact at a company to receive free goods or services? While the obvious answer might be the community relations or corporate giving departments, I found that directly placing a request with the heads of marketing and public relations was the easiest and quickest way to get it considered and approved.

4. What are some local retail stores that have community-service fund-raising programs already in place? Here's where paying attention to signs and marketing materials at retail stores pays off, literally. Both Starbucks and Whole Foods Market, two up-scale and progressive companies, were approached to

donate a percentage of their total sales from one day to the campaign.

With these four questions answered, I got started.

I remembered from my employee manual at the Gap that they donate T-shirts and sweats to charitable organizations. I contacted Gap corporate offices in San Francisco and received five hundred T-shirts. Because I bothered to read their corporate materials, which most people ignored, it was simple to secure the generous gift. I took the T-shirts to a busy Sunday morning flea market, paid $10 for a booth, and sold the shirts at $7 apiece. In less than an hour, I raised $3,500 from T-shirt sales and even collected donations from the public.

I visited Baltimore-area Starbucks stores and Whole Foods Markets and filled out simple paperwork to be eligible for a Five Percent Day. That same month, both retail stores donated five percent of one day's total sales to Habitat for Humanity — and all I had to do was fill out one piece of paper. In less than fifteen minutes, I raised another $3,500. I already achieved more than twenty percent of my goal in less than two hours of work.

I knew how much my friends and I enjoyed eating Wild Oats Community Markets' Belgian chocolate bars, so I contacted the company and asked if they would donate 2,000 bars for my fundraiser. (I think they were impressed that I could rattle off all ten flavors they made.) During my five-minute telephone request, they agreed. I took the chocolates to a busy area in my neighborhood and raised $3,600. At the end of the day, I still had four hundred bars left over, which I donated to a local food collection agency. The agency sold the chocolate and raised an additional $2,000 to assist the hungry of Washington, D.C. Without even trying, I created a mini-miracle for a local charity by donating high-quality confections to their fundraising efforts.

I was watching CNN's *Style with Elsa Klensch* and I got inspired to call big-name fashion designers and retailers like Calvin Klein, Patagonia, and Cynthia Rowley to request showroom pieces. A showroom piece is an article of clothing from a designer's current collection that is borrowed by the media for fashion shoots and kept on hand by the designer for fittings and reference purposes. Once a new collection is ready to be unveiled, these showroom pieces are given away. I collected the unwanted showroom pieces, many of them worth several hundred dollars apiece, and brought them to an upscale Washington, D.C., consignment store for sale. In two weeks, I raised a few thousand dollars.

In less than five hours of work I was able to raise $14,230. And with just a few hours more work, I brought my fund-raising total to more than $30,000. I kept true to my fund-raising philosophy that every fund-raiser I do should be simple, take very little time, and raise lots of money.

In general, my fund-raising philosophy is to keep my eyes open for corporate support and always sell a product that people really need or want and offer it to them at a fair price. It's common sense.

Ten Thousand Dollars in Thirty Days

As a novice fund-raiser, you can raise $10,000 in thirty days or less with these fund-raising ideas. These are my favorite fund-raising ideas and they take very little time and can raise lots of money for your favorite charity.

Book Worn

Ever walk into a bookstore that sells used books and wonder how they make money on a brand-new book—a much-anticipated novel that the national chains don't even carry yet—priced at half the jacket price? Book reviewers at magazines, newspapers, and television stations are flooded with all types of books every week from publishers for review consideration. Since reviewers receive hundreds of books a year, they often sell review copies to bookstores specializing in used merchandise to make extra money.

Contact journalists and producers who receive review copies and ask them to donate one month's supply to your fund-raiser. Ask friends, neighbors, and coworkers to donate used books. Take the books to one of these bookstores (ask about their buying policy ahead of time and set up an appointment if neccessary) and sell the books.

An Unwanted Bake Sale

As much as I enjoy baking, I have no desire to devote an entire weekend to baking 1,000 cookies.

Why bother? Call a local bakery and request that any unsold baked goods be donated to your bake sale. (You can set up a booth at a supermarket or special event—with permission, of course.) Not only will the quality be consistent, you won't feel like you wasted an entire day baking cookies if the sale doesn't take off. After all, all you did was make a phone call and pick up the goods.

Consignment

I admit that not everyone can call a fashion designer and get twenty $700 jackets shipped to them overnight. It's taken me years of networking to develop professional relationships with the designers and their publicity departments. But all of us can raise a lot of money by consigning clothes.

Ask your friends, family, and neighbors to donate good-quality used clothing to your fundraiser. Contact a consignment store in your community and make an appointment to drop off your merchandise and set up an account. In about four weeks, after most of the clothing is sold, you'll receive fifty percent of the money for your worthy cause.

Pennies from Heaven

With thousands of dollars in coins sitting in shopping mall fountains, you'd think savvy fund-raisers would be lining up to collect. Nope.

Who wants to deal with heavy buckets of wet coins? Definitely not me, and you shouldn't either. Place a request for fountain coins with the mall management office. Once approved, contact your local bank's public relations office and request that an armored truck pick up the coins at the mall (or you can pick them up and take them to the bank yourself) and have them shipped to the mutilated coin division (since the coins are wet and slimy) of the U.S. Mint nearest you to be weighed and melted down. The U.S. Mint will send you a check for the amount of the coins within six or eight weeks. You can raise up to $3,000 just by making two phone calls.

Cheap Chic

In my *Oprah* fund-raiser, I asked each member of Congress to make a $10 donation to Habitat for Humanity. I felt that $10 was a fair amount; any less, and it wouldn't raise a lot of money; any more, and our elected officials might have a reason not to give. The fund-raiser was conceived on the spur of the moment; I happened to be lobbying Congress about an environmental law and thought I might as well pass out funding requests at the same time. I drafted a letter, made some photocopies, and — *voila!* — $3,100.

If you work at a large company, ask your coworkers to donate $5 or $10 to your cause. Also, if you live in a neighborhood where everybody knows everybody and you still get together for summer backyard gatherings, you can send out a fund-raising appeal.

Free Tees

This fund-raiser, I admit, is not as simple as the rest. But if you can get approval, the results will be stunning.

My Gap T-shirt fund-raiser was successful. You can achieve similar results by contacting the p.r. department of your favorite clothing retailer and placing a similar request for free T-shirts, too. They may want the request in writing, so have one already typed out before you call and offer to fax it over right away.

Remember, though, that many companies receive more requests than they can possibly fulfill, so you shouldn't be too upset if they turn you down. But if you're fortunate enough to get your request approved, pick a busy place like a flea market to sell the T-shirts at forty percent off the regular retail price. Believe me, once word gets around about your merchandise, it will fly out of there faster than you can say "mini-miracle."

Holiday Splurge

When January 2 rolls around, and the holiday decorations begin to look a little out of place, it's a good time to hit the candy companies.

Let's face it: Very few people are going to walk into a department store and buy old holiday candy, even if it's fifty percent off. Food sitting on a clearance table is just not very tempting.

Ask your favorite candy company, a local one if possible, to donate unwanted holiday candy to your fund-raiser. Take the holiday candy out of the department store environment and bring it to a place where people will want candy, like an office, a busy lunchtime area, or a special event. You'll be surprised how easily the candy will sell.

Percentage Days

One of the easiest and most effective ways to raise funds involves "percentage days" at retail stores. Companies like Wild Oats Community Markets, Starbucks, Barnes & Noble, and Whole Foods Market have designated days each month when they donate five, ten, or even fifteen percent of the total receipts to one charitable organization.

Visit your favorite retail store, like a supermarket or popular bakery, and ask if they'd participate in a similar program. Or just visit a branch of the stores mentioned above and fill out the one-page request.

Free Money

I receive many newsletters each week from worthy causes and I always take the time to read them. In a promotional newsletter for *USA WEEKEND*'s Make a Difference Day, I came across a great program.

Every single Wal-Mart store in America has a program offering $1,000 a year in partnership with Make a Difference Day to support a local charitable project. The request form is pretty standard, asking for your name, what the money will be used for, and a signature. Let me put it this way: I devoted fifteen minutes to filling out two applications and raised $2,000. Visit www.usaweekend.com for more information.

Foundmoney.com

I recently gave $500 to an animal-protection charity. This $500 involved only one minute of my time, on the Internet, and none of my own money. How did I do this? I found lost money for the organization.

Each year, millions of dollars is willed to charitable organizations by people who have died. A lot of this money is left unclaimed due to post office mistakes, address changes, misspelled names, or businesses or banks that have gone bankrupt.

With more than 667,000 charitable organizations in the United States, you can find out if your favorite charity has unclaimed money waiting for it by logging on to the Free Money search engine at www.foundmoney.com.

The search engine will scan an extensive database of lost and unclaimed accounts from government and financial institutions. Unclaimed property in the database includes checking and savings accounts, real estate, certificates of deposit, stocks and bonds, dividends, insurance, utility deposits, safety deposit boxes, and other assets.

If you do track down funds owed to a charitable organization, you can follow the simple steps at foundmoney.com to claim the money for the organization at a cost of just $20. While you're at it, you might as well do a free search for yourself, your friends, and family to locate more lost money. (By the way, I receive absolutely no benefits from promoting this Web site or any other organization or company in this book.)

Heavenly Tips

With more than $143 billion given to charities every year by Americans, there will always be a few unscrupulous individuals who will try to take advantage of your generosity. In fact, according to the Federal Trade Commission, more than one percent, or $1.5 billion, went to charities that either do not meet accepted standards for accounting or are just outright fraudulent.

For these reasons, it's important to follow a few simple tips for giving.

1. Don't make out your check to an organization's initials. J. R. Stevens, a former employee of the Internal Revenue Service, cashed thirteen taxpayer checks worth $77,218 by changing "IRS" on the checks to his name. He simply made the I into a J and added "tevens" after the S. When writing checks to charities, use their full names, not their initials, to make sure the funds go to the organization and not into somebody's pocket.

2. Don't donate used cars to charity. One of the increasingly popular ways to give to a charitable organization is to donate a used car. In my local newspaper, *The Washington Post,* there were more than seven advertisements, most of them from organizations I've never heard of, willing to tow a used car for free to benefit their charity. The truth is that most of these fund-raisers are scams. It's best to sell the car yourself and make a cash contribution to the charity of your choice to really help those who need it most.

3. The American Institute of Philanthropy (AIP) monitors charitable organizations to help the public make informed choices when giving. Their quarterly publication, the *Charity Rating Guide & Watchdog Report,* grades national charities based on the

percentage of their budgets spent for charitable purposes versus the percentage spent for fund-raising purposes. The AIP recommends that sixty percent or more of a charitable organization's annual budget be spent on its mission and that no more than thirty-five percent be spent on fund-raising.

In the AIP's fall 1998 report, grades were given to some popular charities. Please remember that these grades are only the opinions of the AIP, that the AIP does not evaluate the effectiveness of a charity, and that the decision to support a charity ultimately lies with you. (As you'll see, even though Habitat for Humanity didn't earn an A+, I still support it because I know exactly how my money is being spent.) Here are just a few of the charities listed in the report:

Excellent Rating

Big Brothers Big Sisters of America *A*+
Elizabeth Glaser Pediatric AIDS Foundation *A*
American Red Cross *A*
Children's Defense Fund *A*–
People for the Ethical Treatment of Animals *A*–

Good Rating:

Friends of the Earth *B*
National Trust for Historic Preservation *B*
Farm Aid *B–*

Satisfactory Rating:

Habitat for Humanity *C+*
Special Olympics International *C*
Goodwill Industries *C–*

Unsatisfactory Rating:

National Parks and Conservation Association *D*
Mothers Against Drunk Driving *D*
American Institute for Cancer Research *D*

Poor Rating:

Alzheimer's Disease Research *F*
American Heart Disease Prevention Foundation *F*
Feed the Children *F*

Contact the AIP at 4905 Del Ray Avenue, Suite 300, Bethesda, Maryland, 20814, or call (301) 913-5200 for a copy of the report.

4. Refuse point of purchase giving. Ever drop some change into a donation box at the register of your favorite restaurant or at the dry cleaner? Who doesn't have fifty cents to spare here and there to help a starving child or to find a cure for a terminal illness?

The truth about point-of-purchase donation boxes is that the charities that benefit from these collections receive a predetermined amount, sometimes as little as $1.50 per box per month. The rest of the money is given to a profit-making company or individual. It's not against the law, but it sure is unethical and a way of giving you should reject.

Instead, collect your spare change in a jar, and at the end of the month, count it up and write a check to the charity of your choice for that amount.

5. GuideStar is an online guide with reports on more than 650,000 charitable organizations. You can seek out a charity that meets your very specific criteria by searching the online database for organizations based on mission, location, and budget. Plus, you can check GuideStar to make sure a

charity is a legitimate nonprofit organization. Log on at www.guidestar.org.

6. You can deduct your mileage (at fourteen cents per mile) and any out-of-pocket expenses you incur while doing volunteer work from your income taxes, according to the *Ernst & Young Tax Guide 1999.*

7. One of the questions I'm asked most frequently is, "What should I do if a beggar approaches me for money?" When we see human suffering, it's our gut instinct to want to give a dollar or two to try to help. But maybe a friend or family member has warned you that it's better not to give money because it will only be used to buy drugs or alcohol.

Most people ignore panhandlers for a variety of reasons, whether they actually have no money to give or are fearful of the person bothering them. Still, the beggar is ignored.

Whether or not you give money to a homeless person is entirely up to you. But acknowledging his or her existence by saying "I'm all out" or "I have nothing to give this time" is far better than ignoring him or her. These are small gestures, granted, but according to many homeless organizations, they do help give back a measure of self-worth and dignity.

A Review

Do you see how simple it is to double your contribution to charity and raise large sums of money quickly and easily?

You can give double what you normally donate without actually having to give more from your own pocket. You can raise large sums of money in very little time with very little work. And what you receive in return is priceless: your spiritual well-being will improve, you'll feel true joy, and you'll see your life begin to change for the better.

TEN MINI-MIRACLES YOU CAN DO TO CHANGE YOUR WORLD

1. Register with www.igive.com, an online shopping mall that donates up to 12.5 percent of the value of the purchases you make at their Web site to the charity of your choice. You don't even need to buy anything to have a donation made in your name; spend a few minutes to register as

a free member, and igive.com will make a one-time donation of two dollars to your favorite charity. It's quick and easy and helps a nonprofit organization raise money.

2. The next time you reply to a fund-raising appeal and the charity promises to send you "a free gift for your donation," enclose a note with your check asking them to keep the free gift. The organization saves money by keeping the premium and can use every penny you give to create even more mini-miracles.

3. Put in your "two cents" about personal finance management and hot stock tips at www.fool.com, and raise money for Share Our Strength, the nation's leading anti-hunger organization, at the same time. During The Motley Fool's annual charity drive, they'll donate two cents for each message posted on their Web site. While that may not sound like much, if you post ten messages and 50,000 others do the same, that's $10,000 for a good cause.

4. On Halloween, encourage your children to go door-to-door collecting candy for themselves and money for UNICEF, the children's advocacy division of the United Nations. Call UNICEF at

(212) 686-5522 for more information or write them at 333 East 38th Street, New York, New York 10016.

5. If you're a Discover cardholder, donate your cash back bonus to the charity of your choice.

6. Many long distance telephone companies are now offering up-front cash payments if you switch to their long distance calling plan. Recently, one company offered me $50 cash if I switched. Not only did I get a good deal on my long distance, but I cashed the check and donated the money to a worthy cause (and got a tax deduction).

7. Lots of companies are proud of their community spirit. "Ten percent of all proceeds benefit charity" is a commonly found phrase on tubes of toothpaste, bottles of pasta sauce, or cartons of ice cream. If you buy products from a generous company, call their toll-free customer service number and suggest a charity or two that you'd like to see them support with that ten percent.

8. Double the amount of toys you donate to Toys for Tots, the United States Marine Corps's premier community service program, without having to spend a dime more. Beginning November 1 every

year, buy toys online at eToys, the Internet's top toy store, purchase toys online with a Visa card, and save fifty percent off retail when donating toys to Toys for Tots. In 1998, more than 15,000 toys were donated; visit www.etoys.com and make it an annual tradition.

9. If you shop at a supermarket that participates in monthly Five Percent Days—a special day each month when five percent of the day's total sales benefit a local charity—shop on that day. Not only can you finish your grocery shopping for the week, but you and others shopping that day will have raised thousands of dollars for a good cause.

10. If you belong to a charitable organization that sends you a monthly or quarterly magazine or newsletter, and you receive duplicate copies, notify the organization and ask them to fix the mailing problem. Not only is this an ecologically sound thing to do, but it also saves the charity money.

I BELIEVE CHILDREN ARE THE PRESENT

*Nothing is more powerful than
an individual acting out of his conscience,
thus helping to bring the collective conscience to life.*

— NORMAN COUSINS

Nothing matters more than our children.

Whether you're a married parent with three young children, a single mother with a ten-year-old aspiring soccer star, or you have no children of your own, it is your responsibility—and mine—to protect, to guide, and to mentor children into compassionate, caring, well-adjusted members of society. Children, after all, are the future. The harder we work today with children, the better they will be able to thrive as adults in the future.

When you started this book, you embarked on a journey to seek out a more fulfilling life for yourself by helping others. Now I urge you to take the next step: Guide a child on this path as well.

By exposing children to the power of helping others, you'll not only show them that they matter and they truly can make a difference but you may also help them discover the joy of kindness and compassion.

The work of young leaders like Jon Wagner-Holtz, David Levitt, and Amber Coffman can give us valuable insight into what inspires and drives youth to selflessly give. We can use that insight to help inspire other young people to change the world.

Miracle Worker: Jon Wagner-Holtz

I met Jon Wagner-Holtz at the 1998 *react* magazine Take Action Awards. He was selected as one of five award recipients for his work as the CEO and founder of Kids Konnected, Inc., a cancer support group for young people. When he was just sixteen years old, Jon had already sold his life story to a movie production company, had more frequent-flier miles than any business road warrior, and was planning his retirement.

Jon's amazing story began when he was eleven years old and his mother developed breast cancer. He had difficulty dealing with his mother's illness and was sent to a psychologist, who basically told him to "cheer up and think positively." "I realized there was nothing available to the youth of America who had a parent with cancer," Jon explains. He decided to start his own organization to help other kids like him.

Jon's mother doubted that he would stick with the idea. "I said to him, 'You know, if you're going to do this, you have to be committed, because I'm not doing it for you.'" She was sure that Jon would stay with it for "a month at most" and then "forget it." He was just a kid, after all.

But Jon was determined to make it work. He networked and spoke to people about the idea. He decided to start a hot line in his home so that "kids could call us twenty-four hours a day, seven days a week, to answer questions, share concerns, or just listen." Jon asked the Susan G. Komen Breast Cancer Foundation for a $283 grant to get a phone line installed, print flyers, and buy postage stamps. Often, it was just Jon and his friends who answered calls and offered advice and an ear to concerned kids. To his surprise, the hot line took off, helping hundreds of young people deal with the trauma of a parent with cancer. And just as Jon's mother recovered from her cancer, Kids Konnected chapters sprang up around the country.

Today, Kids Konnected boasts eighteen chapters in twelve states and an annual budget of $150,000—all the result of a $283 seed grant. Recently, Vice President Al Gore told a conference of health care professionals that Jon's organization was a model of financial efficiency. "We give all you health care professionals three million dollars to start, and look at this kid who received two hundred bucks," Jon recounts the Vice President as saying.

Jon has big plans for the future, including a personal goal of becoming the youngest

United States Congressman. His immediate goal, though, is to train a young member of the board of directors to take over as CEO when he leaves for college. "It's really important to continue Kids Konnected as a corporation that is run by kids, for kids," he says.

When children discover a reason to care and take action, they are capable of feats that are nothing short of extraordinary. By actively giving their time and energy to further a cause, they demonstrate a desire to be selfless. And when young people learn the value of being selfless, their own leadership, critical thinking, and problem-solving skills will strengthen. Down the road, when they are starting careers and raising families of their own, these skills will contribute to a life for them that glows with self-confidence and success.

Miracle Worker: David Levitt

When David Levitt of Pinellas County, Florida, was eleven years old, he learned about the Jewish tradition of *tzedaka,* or the act of giving, at his weekly Sunday school class. David was so inspired by the class that he decided to practice what he had learned by giving back to his own community.

Later that day, he was flipping through a copy of *Parade* when he was struck by a story about USA Harvest, a food collection organization. This article gave David the idea of trying to help feed those who were hungry in his community. But like most good-hearted people, he didn't know how.

A few days later, his school cafeteria was throwing away cartons of milk, sandwiches, and other food that had gone unpurchased. Why couldn't that food instead be donated to help feed the hungry in his community? David wondered. This seemed like such an obvious and easy way to help fight hunger, and David approached his principal to ask if this would be possible.

David was surprised at the response. "The principal said that he thought they couldn't do it; he was sure there were laws and regulations on the state level against giving food," he said. What if the food spoiled? Who would be liable if someone got ill from eating a bad sandwich or drinking spoiled milk? David explained it a little more bluntly: "Too much red tape."

When David learned his idea had been turned down, he asked his mother what else they could do. "She said we could go to the school board and ask," he said. So the two sat down and wrote a letter to the school board explaining why it wouldn't be harmful to donate food. To their surprise, the school board approved the idea. "I was shocked," said David. Because David had taken his simple idea to the school board and made a very clear case why his was a good idea, he was able to convince the board to donate food not just from his school but from all ninety-two schools in the county. "We were expecting them to say no, but they didn't," adds Sandy, David's mother. On November 10, 1993, David's idea became a school policy that brought nourishing food to hungry people in his community.

And his good deeds didn't go unnoticed. That year, David was given the Presidential Service Award by First Lady Hillary Clinton.

And while most young miracle workers would be satisfied with a job well done, he wanted to do more. So when a radio disc jockey jokingly asked him during an interview why he hadn't yet written a state law requiring all schools across the state of Florida to give food to the needy, he turned to his mother and asked, "How do you do that?"

David's parents suggested he pay a visit to state legislator Dennis Jones to see if he could help. Representative Jones asked David to write down everything he thought should be in the law and he would "put all of that legal jargon in." In a few months, the bill finally came up for vote.

Unlike the district-wide school policy, however, this idea didn't pass with flying colors. Because the bill lacked a senate supporter to guide it through the complicated legislative process, it was ignored in the senate despite passing in the house. The setback didn't upset David. He simply accepted defeat and decided to try again the following year.

In 1997, state senator Charlie Crist wrote David after reading a newspaper article about him, and offered to help in any way possible. Perfect timing, David thought. Now, with Senator Crist spearheading the bill through the senate, it had a greater chance to pass into law. But the detail-oriented Senator Crist, with David's permission, wanted to improve the bill; he knew it could be stronger.

In Florida, the Good Samaritan Law protects the giver and the receiver of donated food from liability, but it didn't protect those who transported the food. This didn't make sense to the senator or to David, and they believed if the parties that transport donated food were also protected from liability, then more commercial and nonprofit institutions would donate food. This way, a school or hotel couldn't fear liability from being generous.

On May 28, 1998, when David was working as a page for the senator, his new and improved bill came up for vote on the senate floor. This was an exciting day for David, not just because the bill was up for vote, but because David made Florida legislative history. David was the first non-elected person ever to address the state senate from the floor;

he provided a moving and convincing speech that ultimately persuaded the Florida senate to pass the bill.

Now, across Florida, schools, food producers, restaurants, hotels, and any businesses that create large amounts of food are free of any liability if they donate food to the hungry. Because of this tenacious teenage miracle worker, there are thousands of hungry people who now receive nourishing food across the entire state of Florida.

It was tough to track down David when I wanted to interview him for this book; his schedule began at 5:00 A.M. with homework and ended at 10:00 P.M., when rehearsals for his school play were over for the day. David, of course, had the lead role.

When David's request to have his school donate food to the hungry was rejected, he learned a very important lesson: Perseverance is so important not only to help others but also to succeed and to thrive in life. If David hadn't believed unconditionally in his idea, thousands of people in his state would still be hungry.

Miracle Worker: Amber Coffman

When Amber Coffman of Glen Burnie, Maryland, was just eight years old, her mother wanted to spend some meaningful time with her daughter. "My mother wanted to do something valuable with her time also, so she asked me if it was okay if we worked at a homeless shelter," says the sixteen-year-old activist. Her mother thought helping the community could help them bond.

"I was hesitant to volunteer; I didn't know what to expect. I thought it would be scary." After mulling over her mom's idea for a few days, Amber decided to go. She's happy now that she did, because the experience changed her life. "I flipped over it. I worked with the homeless kids, and the kids were just like me. You couldn't tell they were homeless. I had an awesome time." She continued to volunteer with her mother every weekend, cooking food and helping the kids sort clothes. But she felt underutilized and wanted to affect the lives of more people.

Like other miracle workers profiled in this book, Amber wanted to accomplish more, but "didn't know how." It wasn't until she wrote a school book report on Mother Teresa that Amber found her inspiration. "I realized there were people on the streets who were cold and hungry all the time, but I couldn't provide shelter for them. I could, however, provide lunches, love, and care for the people." Excited about her plan to help those less fortunate in her community, Amber founded Happy Helpers for the Homeless. "Our emphasis is to provide lunches for the homeless and show people that we love and care for them," says Amber. Ever since the day she started Happy Helpers for the Homeless, she's stayed committed to her promise to help.

Every Friday, Amber meets with local supermarkets and fast-food restaurants to receive free food donations for her organization. Even though many places turned her down initially, she used her youthfulness to win them over. "My age really helps because nobody can say no to someone this young," Amber says. And it's her age and savvy that have helped her collect a tremendous amount of food, like 20,000 slices of cheese and 27,000 hamburger buns that would have normally been tossed away.

Every Saturday morning, Amber's friends come over to her family's small apartment and prepare lunches in the living room. They make hundreds of complete meals that include a sandwich, fresh fruit, a snack, and a beverage. Then in the evening, the group piles into a Happy Helper car (she convinced a local car dealer to donate it) and distributes the meals to hundreds of "people who need to be loved." These energetic teens wake up bright and early on Sunday and repeat the whole process again; since she started Happy Helpers in 1993, Amber has not missed a weekend of helping.

What keeps a teenager like Amber motivated and dedicated to serving her community for five years in a row? "It's where my heart is at. I don't see myself doing anything else. I don't feel like I'm giving up too much, just gaining so much; I get a wonderful feeling inside because I'm making a day a little brighter."

Amber's dedication even caught the attention of her role model. In 1997, Mother Teresa invited Amber to come to India and assist her in helping the poor. Unfortunately, before Amber could accept her invitation, Mother Teresa passed away. It was a sad day for Amber, but she still holds on to the letter from Mother Teresa. Being acknowledged by her was one of the "greatest moments of my life," Amber says. The compassion and kindness of Mother Teresa, without a doubt, lives on in Amber's dedicated work.

Amber's dream is to someday be the director of a homeless shelter. She has learned that she has the potential to change the world. But to devote her life to serving others, she needs a college education. Using the marketing skills and savvy she's pulled from running her own organization, she has raised enough scholarship money to attend a four-year college of her choice, for free. She set her eyes on a goal and got it.

The Core Traits of Kids Who Care

Once children discover the joy in helping others, they will develop traits associated with kids who care.

Over the last three years, I have interviewed fifty extraordinary young leaders to uncover their sources of inspiration and motivation, what their future goals are, and how they feel about different social issues facing their generation. In my unscientific study, I discovered:

1. Many young leaders are either ranked in the top five percent or the bottom ten percent of their secondary-school class. Some superachieving philanthropists who see the value of working hard apply those same skills to their academic lives. Other young leaders, who may be drafting their own state legislation, for example, or serving on White House panels addressing global issues, perform horribly in a school setting. "The environment doesn't encourage critical thinking," Maurice Olsen, a young environmental activist, said. Unlike some other young people who perform poorly in school,

however, young leaders who make a difference in the world have little difficulty succeeding in a real-world environment because of their ability to adapt to life's difficulties and find a way to persevere.

Young people who have real-world experience in helping others can gain confidence, knowledge, and contacts with high-profile leaders in government and business. Their skills can help them succeed beyond their altruistic work to become mavericks in their careers of choice, regardless of class rank.

2. Young leaders do not drink alcohol, smoke cigarettes, or experiment with illicit drugs. They also do not look down on those who do. Young people who embrace compassion see the value of life and understand the dangers of unhealthful activities. They also realize that using drugs would interfere with charitable work.

3. Young leaders do not depend on their parents as much as their peers do. Teenagers who engage in service projects rely less on their parents for support as they create a place for themselves in the world. At a recent State of the World Forum conference in San Francisco, young "emerging leaders" acknowledged that they initiate, launch, and finish their charitable work on their own. This attitude of

responsibility shows up in other aspects of their lives as well.

4. Young leaders absorb information like a sponge and apply it to real-life experiences and situations. Young leaders are constantly seeking new sources of information to enhance their problem-solving abilities, their critical thinking skills, and to streamline and improve their work. They read books on a myriad of subjects out of a desire to better themselves and to strengthen their own critical thinking abilities.

5. Young leaders have confidence, self-esteem, and a clear vision of what the future holds for them. Young people who embrace service pull valuable lessons from their leadership roles and network with other young leaders. Melissa Poe founded Kids for a Clean Environment when she was eleven years old and turned it into a 600,000-member environmental group; by her fifteenth birthday, she had set her eyes on becoming the first woman President of the United States. While many would think she's just being idealistic, she doesn't think so. There's a Melissa Poe for President fund already in existence.

We all know that being selfless can make someone a better person. To get a person excited about volunteerism at an early age not only helps him or her learn how to be kind and generous, it's also a step toward helping that young person mature into a successful, well-rounded, contributing member of society.

Conveniently Placed Inspiration

Here are some suggestions for helping children discover a reason to care and for providing moments of inspiration for them.

Volunteer

Jon Wagner-Holtz's mother said that ever since her children were old enough to walk, they helped volunteer for groups like Meals on Wheels. "They saw that when we volunteer and give back, they would slowly take on responsibilities of their own."

The next time you volunteer at a senior center, a hospital, or soup kitchen, invite your children along to help. Keep the kids close to you, and ask them to assist you by doing small tasks. Don't create busywork projects for them; make them an essential link in the volunteer activity. Also, tell them that if at any point they feel uncomfortable or scared, they can ask to leave. It's important to make sure kids don't feel that volunteering is a chore; rather, it should be an activity they want to do.

Television

While television is often blamed for corrupting the young with sex, foul language, and violence, it can also be a useful educational tool.

When I was sixteen years old, the news program *20/20* inspired me to launch an international campaign to protect the Faeroe Islands pilot whales.

Correspondent Lynn Sherr reported how the residents of the Faeroe Islands, a small island colony in the North Atlantic, killed thousands of pilot whales annually in the "name of tradition." I was outraged. Not only were the killings brutal and gruesome to watch, they were also unnecessary: Perhaps hundreds of years ago, the native islanders needed the whale meat to survive. But given the island's high standard of living, which includes luxury cars and high-tech equipment, I felt it was senseless slaughter.

I made the pilot whales campaign a top priority for Earth 2000. After six months of campaigning, which included extensive letter-writing, a United Kingdom Faeroese seafood boycott, and a high-profile protest in Washington, D.C., worldwide attention was brought to the Faeroe Islands. And I owe it all to the power of television.

When your children are old enough, encourage them to watch the nightly news or a newsmagazine program like *Dateline NBC*. While television news may be more sensational than it used to be, it can still help educate your children about their own communities and the world around them.

Newspapers

One of the most effective ways to inspire young people is to expose them to newspapers.

Clip human-interest stories, calendar announcements of upcoming volunteer activities, or articles about a global problem or serious social issue and post them on the bulletin board, refrigerator, or drop them in your children's lunch bag. Encourage them to read the materials and tell you what they think.

Magazine Subscriptions

There are some great publications that can help kids discover the power of altruism on a rainy day. Choose one of the following and have it sent to your child or a neighborhood kid (kids love to receive mail).

react is a news and entertainment magazine for teens that is distributed weekly in certain newspapers and in classrooms across the country. In their Everyday Heroes section, the magazine profiles amazing young people doing things to improve their communities and sponsors the *react* Take Action Awards, a national awards program that recognizes young people actively changing the world. Surf *react* at www.react.com or call (800) 58-REACT to find out which newspapers carry it.

blue jean is an alternative to the beauty and glamour–focused magazines targeted at young people; the magazine profiles real young women on the verge of changing the world. Call (888) 4-BLU-JEAN or visit www.bluejeanmag.com for more information.

Fox Kids Magazine — While this magazine mostly covers — what else — programs on the Fox television network, it does carry a monthly column profiling the community service work of amazing young people. Visit www.foxkids.com for more information.

Giving Thanks

It wasn't until one Thanksgiving when I was sixteen years old, and I was having dinner at a friend's house that I discovered the American tradition of "giving thanks." I was amazed that my friend's family followed the practice of giving thanks for one's health, one's family, and, as one family member put it, "because Bloomingdale's had my sweater, in my size, at half price."

Many people believe that "giving thanks" on a regular basis helps kids develop a greater appreciation for the necessities of life that are so easily taken for granted—basics like having a roof over their heads, clothing to keep them warm, and food to eat.

Before dinner, encourage your children to give thanks for something in their lives. This moment of reflection at dinnertime can remind them that others go without food, without shelter, and without being loved, and that through volunteering they can help make a difference.

Troubleshooting

As tempting as it may be, "guilting" a child into taking action doesn't work. If you make children feel guilty for not caring, for only being concerned about getting the latest toys or clothing, or for not helping the community, they will view volunteerism negatively. "Excessive guilt," says sixteen-year-old activist Sarah Wilson, "prevented me from doing anything for a long time. I felt like I was offending everyone and couldn't do anything because my mom and dad made me feel so bad when I was young."

Instead of guilting them into action, rephrase your approach. "How would you feel if we spent next Saturday morning taking canned food to the food bank? I could really use your help." This is far better than, "How can you not care about people who are hungry in this country?"

Stage Parents

There's a fine line between creating mini-miracles with a child and coaching a child to be a miracle worker. To avoid philanthropic-stage-parent syndrome, it is absolutely imperative that a child decide when she would like to help, how she would like to help, and whether she's ready to progress to more challenging mini-miracles down the road. It will always be the child's call; your job is to guide her in the right direction.

A couple of years ago, a *Family Circle* writer interviewed my parents for a feature article on "superachieving" teens. The goal of the article was to gain insight into the "innovative parenting skills" my mother and father had. What were these magical skills? Absolutely nothing.

Very early on, my parents realized that it was important for me to achieve my own successes and learn from my mistakes and failures. The feeling from my father was, "Well, if you're going to go off and start an organization, you succeed and fail at your own expense." My parents decided that they wouldn't interfere with my work unless I asked them to help and so I learned to take responsibility for my own actions at a very early age.

When I tell people that my parents didn't get involved with my early philanthropic work, they look back at me with pity. They think it's sad my parents didn't help me raise money and campaign to protect historical forests. The truth is, I'm glad they weren't involved.

If my parents had given financial support to my organization, run my campaigns, or even helped draft some of my first lectures, I wouldn't have made so many mistakes, but I also wouldn't have been able to learn and to grow from them. And every time that I succeeded, I knew that I could take credit for my own hard work and perseverance.

My parents are without a doubt proud of me. But the fact that they intentionally stepped back from my early work helped me to develop my drive and made me want to be a better person because I desired to, not because someone else pushed me to. And for that, I am grateful.

Always allow children to feel they're in control of their volunteer activities. When you volunteer with them, rather than saying "Here, do this," say, "What do you think we should do next to help?" If they don't know, offer choices and let them decide. By allowing children to use their own intuitive problem-solving skills, they will feel integral to the work and grow less reliant on others for help.

Volunteering

There are hundreds of volunteer opportunities that you and your child can take advantage of together or with the entire family. A weekend of helping others can not only improve your community but can also can teach invaluable lessons to your kids about love, service, and mercy on a firsthand basis in a real-world classroom.

Try to find a volunteer activity that will be exciting and fulfilling for both of you. Be choosy. Take the time to call organizations, ask questions, and—at all times—keep your child involved in the process.

Some places to approach when looking for a volunteer activity are listed below.

Volunteer Centers

There are volunteer centers in almost every city and community in the United States. These resource centers can help you pinpoint the right volunteer activity for you and your child. For a complete list, please see the resource directory in the back of the book or visit www.pointsoflight.org on the World Wide Web.

The Government

Local government offices run volunteer coordination programs that help families find service opportunities that match their child's age, the family's interests, and your time availability. Many volunteer coordination offices offer thousands of volunteer job opportunities and information on hundreds of nonprofit and government agencies seeking volunteer support.

The YMCA

The YMCA is more than a place to get fit. Many YMCA centers around the country have community-service programs that help families serve their community. Contact your local YMCA for volunteer activities in your area.

Hands-On National Volunteer Groups

Organizations like Habitat for Humanity and the Center for Marine Conservation (CMC) organize community-wide events that depend on volunteers. CMC, for example, sponsors an annual cleanup that rallies communities around the world to remove debris from the shorelines, waterways, and beaches of the world's lakes, rivers, and oceans. Data on the debris is recorded, providing valuable information on the quantity and types of litter piling up on our beaches and in our waterways.

Places of Worship

Most churches, synagogues, and temples have committees devoted to community-service activities. Most organize youth activities that, for example, bake cookies for senior citizens, bring food to shut-ins, or raise money for charitable causes.

Advocacy Groups

If you have a shy child who doesn't want to be out in public doing hands-on work, he can volunteer to do administrative projects for a charitable group. Basic office tasks, like stuffing envelopes or making photocopies, teach efficiency and teamwork skills as well.

Special Events

Not-for-profit special events around the country, like Earth Day festivals and free music concerts in the park, are always in need of volunteers to man booths, sell tickets, set up props, and so on. While this may not be as results-oriented as painting a graffiti-covered wall, it can still be a fun and worthwhile project for the family. Besides, the perks aren't so bad; often, concerts headlined by big-name musicians give free backstage passes to volunteers.

The day a child comes up to you and says "I want to do something to help" should be one of the greatest moments of your life. In a culture that embraces consumerism and instant gratification rather than gratitude and compassion, the child that says this has chosen to embrace something more.

Everyday Mini-Miracles—For Kids!

For families and children who cannot make regular volunteer commitments to one charitable organization, but would still like to get involved, fifteen-minute mini-miracles can be the solution. Here are ten mini-miracles kids can do before or after school, on the weekends, or during summer vacation.

1. Gather unwanted but salable items from around the home, like clothing, books, and toys, for fifteen minutes every night for a whole week. Hold a yard sale on the weekend and donate the proceeds to a favorite charity.

2. Donate old children's videos to a homeless shelter so disadvantaged kids can watch them.

3. Have your kids pick out hats at the store and donate them to the American Cancer Society, which will give them to children who have lost their hair due to chemotherapy. Children recovering in the hospital can choose from a selection of hats. Call (800) ACS-2345 for more information.

4. If your child feels upset about something he reads in the newspaper, help him draft a letter to the editor to express his views.

5. Put your child in charge of recycling and make it her responsibility to keep recyclables out of the trash and ready for pickup on the designated day.

6. Invite your kids to join you in asking the neighborhood to donate canned food for a food bank. Send a letter to neighbors asking if they'd like

to donate some food; collect the food and make a field trip with the kids to the food bank. Take a tour of the food bank after you drop off the food.

7. Ask your child to donate one toy from his holiday wish list to Toys for Tots, the Marine Corps Reserve campaign to collect toys for needy children around the United States. Since 1947, more than 116 million children have received new toys during the holiday season through the Toys for Tots program.

8. Write an E-mail letter with your children to your elected officials. The kids can outline their concerns and ask the politicians what they're doing to help. Be sure to ask for a reply. This is a great lesson in civics for kids. Visit the League of Women Voters Web site at www.lwv.org.

9. If you've got pennies, nickels, dimes, and quarters sitting in cookie jars and piggy banks, bring them to a Coinstar change counting machine. The bright green machines automatically calculate how much change you have and convert it into paper money. Donate the money to your children's favorite charity. Call (800) 644-2646 to locate a Coinstar machine near you, or visit www.coinstar.com.

10. If your child wants to join a national organization, pay the membership fee. When children feel

that they are a needed part of a movement to help others or the world, they see the value in belonging and trying to make a difference.

Six Ways to Keep Kids Inspired

Kids have short attention spans. One minute, they'll desperately want a toy and promise to play with it all the time. You know what happens if you buy it: It ends up under the bed, untouched and ignored, just hours later.

You can prevent short attention spans by keeping children inspired and motivated. If they see concrete results from their mini-miracle work, they'll *want* to do more. A quick spark of inspiration could be enough to ignite a world of good from your child.

1. And the winner is... Make sure your child knows how proud and appreciative you are of her hard work. Take the time to notice and to encourage her accomplishments, no matter how small, and reward her with praise for a job well done.

2. Make it adventurous. If you're planning a vacation to a faraway destination, organize a one-

day volunteer activity in the city you're visiting. Don't tell your kids you're taking a vacation, but instead announce you're going on an adventure. For example, tell the kids you're going to help build a Habitat for Humanity home in Florida for a day or two, and as their reward for helping, the family will spend the day at Disney World.

3. Ask for a solution. Don't just make the kids *feel* integral to a volunteer activity; make them *be* integral. Constantly ask your child for her input on the right way to approach an activity, whether it be which cups to use at the soup kitchen or what color paper should be placed into the photocopier.

4. Show confidence in them. When you exude self-confidence, it shows kids how to have confidence in themselves. Self-respect and self-confidence go hand in hand and will be key in your child's ability to be successful in all aspects of his life.

5. Keep it fun. Helping others and making a difference in the world should never be a chore or a bore. Keep volunteer activities exciting for the child, so they're seen as a fun and fulfilling.

6. Be a role model. When I was growing up, I would watch my mother pay the bills every week. From observing her, I learned that when a bill

arrives, you pay it right away. To this day, I cannot let a day go by without paying my bills immediately.

When Amber Coffman's mother brought her daughter to volunteer at a homeless shelter, the experience changed her life. Because her mother was a role model to her daughter as a committed volunteer, Amber evolved into a young leader helping the less fortunate all over the world.

Put Your Daughter to Work

The third Thursday in April is a special day for millions of girls who team up with parents, relatives, neighbors, and friends and take part in the popular Take Our Daughters to Work Day. The purpose of the event is to focus on girls' ideas, needs, and dreams and to help ensure that girls remain confident and strong in school through their teen years. During the day, the girls get hands-on experience and exposure to different opportunities in the business world. This boosts their self-esteem and helps them understand the pressures their parents face in a work environment.

Participation in Take Our Daughters to Work Day is easy. All you need to do is ask a girl in your life—a daughter, granddaughter, niece, neighbor, or friend—if she would like to go with you to your workplace for the day. Since more than one-third of American companies participate, and seventy-five percent of all Americans have heard of Take Our Daughters to Work Day, it shouldn't be difficult to find support from schools or your workplace to take part.

What about boys? Boys have their own developmental needs. The Fatherhood Project in New York offers a lesson plan designed for boys to coincide with Take Our Daughters to Work Day that addresses stereotypes of manliness and the importance of mentoring and caregiving. You can order the kit, called Especially for Boys, from The Fatherhood Project (see the resource guide for contact information).

Mentor a Child

If you do not have children of your own, one of the greatest things you can do to help a child is to become a mentor. When you mentor a child, you become his compass, directing him to his fullest potential.

The statistics supporting mentoring are impressive. According to Big Brothers Big Sisters, young people with mentors are

- forty-six percent less likely to start using drugs;
- twenty-seven percent less likely to start drinking alcohol;
- thirty-three percent less likely to hit someone;
- fifty-two percent less likely to skip a day of school.

What Is a Mentor?

What is a mentor? Look over the definitions below and circle the ones that describe what a mentor is, and cross out the ones that describe what a mentor isn't.

1. A trusted friend
2. A savior
3. A foster parent
4. A guide
5. A good listener
6. A responsive adult
7. A therapist

8. A reliable adult
9. A parole officer
10. A cool peer

The ones that describe what a mentor is are numbers 1, 4, 5, 6, and 8. As you can see, mentoring is not a difficult thing to do; all you have to be is a responsible adult to assist a young person through life. A mentor is a wise and trusted friend. Responsible mentoring is a structured one-to-one relationship or partnership that focuses on the needs of a young person, fosters caring and supportive relationships, encourages young people to develop to their fullest potential, and helps a young person to develop his or her own vision for the future. There is, however, a bit of training you need to go through before becoming a mentor. It's simple to do but the effects are powerful.

Training to be a mentor does take more than fifteen minutes. A training process includes a short written application, personal and professional references, a background check for criminal activities, and a personal interview. It may take a while to be matched with a child. The application, screening, and training can take from one to six months to complete. Mentoring programs are concerned with the well-being and safety of children and mentoring volunteers, and their selection and screening procedures reflect these concerns.

For "Sweet" Alice Harris the power of mentoring is nothing new.

Miracle Worker: "Sweet" Alice Harris

Alice Harris is distracted during my interview with her. Children are running around her office, staff members ask her to sign papers, and she's keeping a "close eye" on a volunteer and a teenage boy playing basketball outside her office window.

"A young man, age fourteen, said to me that he didn't want to go to public school," Alice explains. "He said he could not read or write." This was an emergency situation to Alice; so much so that she put everything on hold to help this young man. Just minutes earlier, Alice had called a male volunteer into her office and said, "I want you to make this kid feel good, as if he is at home and has a friend. Develop his self-esteem." So they're playing basketball. "Once this child feels good about himself, then I say to him, 'Son, you must go to school. I can't let you come here. You go to school and we'll watch you and help you because you have a friend here.'" She assigns a mentor to him, tells him he is welcome at the center any time he wants, and gives him a hug. It's just another typical day for "Sweet" Alice Harris.

Alice Harris lives and works in the Watts section of Los Angeles, the infamous neighborhood remembered as the site of the 1965 riots described as the bloodiest in American history. All her life, Alice Harris had been told that children growing up in this neighborhood didn't have a chance to make it in life. She didn't buy it. So in 1965, all by herself, in the kitchen of her own home, she set up an organization called Parents of Watts (POW) to help people in need in her community. Word soon spread, neighbors came out to help, donations slowly poured in, and Alice forged ahead. In 1982, POW moved into a permanent community center in the middle of Watts. It was a proud day for Alice.

POW is different from other neighborhood assistance centers. "We create a thirst so that people who need our help will want to drink. Nobody wants help if they don't want it. We give them an environment where we'll help them any way that they need help...diaper a baby, find a job, teach a child how to read."

POW assists homeless people, provides emergency food and housing, registers people to vote, hosts health seminars, and offers employment services. Homeless people living at the shelter are put to work. "We aren't running a motel here," says Alice, the mother of nine children and a new grandmother. The homeless men and women do laundry, clean the grounds, and maintain a garden in exchange for having a place to sleep, eat, and learn valuable job skills.

Even though this miracle work alone is extraordinary, Alice's passionate mission is to help the children of Watts.

In the summer, when young people are most likely to commit crimes or get into trouble, POW offers classes to young people in English, math, photography, and parenting skills. The children are also assigned a mentor for life, helping them make it through the difficulties of adolescence, especially in a dangerous neighborhood like Watts.

These adult mentors help kids do their homework, teach them about avoiding drugs, register them to vote, help them fill out college applications, get scholarships, even help them get a haircut and new clothing—anything that will assist them in making it through life. And these "loser" kids *are* bucking the odds: They're attending college and advancing in the workplace.

In just one tiny example of Alice's astonishing accomplishments, in 1985 she secured forty scholarships so that forty teenagers from Watts could attend Morristown College in Morristown, Tennessee, for free. "Oh, I don't think about my achievements," says Alice. "I worry that I'll think I've done enough, even though there is still so much to do." Since 1965, she's helped more than 6,000 kids.

The secret to helping at-risk youth, says Alice, is to build up their self-esteem. That can mean playing basketball with them or doing something else to make them feel special. But making sure kids feel special can be tough. In 1995, Alice decided that one way to accomplish this would be to build a special place the kids could go to feel good about themselves. She decided to build a mansion. But when others questioned the idea, saying they couldn't spend money on an expensive building, especially a mansion, Alice didn't flinch. "Not a problem," she said.

Alice recruited twelve ex-prisoners to build the home and had them trained by a contractor. Supplemented with a few dozen volunteers, they hammered and sawed every single day. Just a year and a half later, the magnificent 10,000-square-foot mansion was completed. "God helps you do the impossible," Alice says.

In addition to holding meetings and special events there, Alice makes good on her promise to help kids feel good about themselves. The kids dress up in rented evening gowns and tuxedos and feel special. "We throw them a party and give them the chance to show themselves off and make them know that they're somebody. This might be their only chance to go to a big party." How can a party in a mansion possibly help kids? "It takes love. These kids need to belong and they need to feel like they are wanted. When you show love, that's all they need," she explains. If the children feel needed, special, and loved, then the mansion was definitely a wise investment in building these kids' futures.

Before our interview ends, Alice tells me that "Some woman, oh, I don't know...uh... oh, yeah, Whoopi Goldberg, bought the rights to my life story." I ask her what it's like to have a big celebrity thinking of making a movie of her life. She's distracted; the mentor playing basketball with the teenage boy comes in to tell Alice to look at the expression on the young boy's face. She looks out the window and sees he's happy. She gives a loud hoot and thanks the volunteer for a job well done.

I meet hundreds of amazing people every year, and even in that crowd, Alice stands out. Alice had to fight the stereotype that kids growing up in the Watts neighborhood didn't have a decent chance in life. Alice gives kids a chance for a better life through mentoring and fights to keep the Watts neighborhood as healthy and nurturing as possible for them.

Your Mentoring Experience

When you were a child, did somebody take time out of his or her life to help you? To help you with homework? Tell you about the dangers of drugs? Help you get into the college of your choice? You can do the same for one of fifteen million at-risk youth today, sharing your skills and support so that they can make it in life, too.

It's important that we encourage at-risk youth early so that we can give them the confidence, skills, and support they will need to make their dreams a reality. As an adult mentor, you can do small things, like take them to work for a day, spend a Saturday afternoon helping them with homework, or just be a friend playing basketball.

When you mentor young people, you play an active role in shaping their lives by encouraging them to strive for success. You improve their self-image, get them excited about life, and teach them marketable real-world skills that foster the growth of their own critical thinking and problem-solving abilities.

Before you contact a mentoring organization to get involved, ask yourself:

- What activities and skills can I offer to help make a connection to a young person?
- What age and number of kids would I prefer to work with; would I prefer working with a child on a one-to-one basis or coaching an entire team of kids?
- How much time can I give?

You should remember that mentoring is a major commitment; it's more than a fifteen-minute mini-miracle. As with any charitable project, you are free to end a mentoring relationship if you are unable to mentor anymore. But before becoming a mentor, just be honest with yourself—for everyone's sake. If you don't have the time and energy to mentor a young person, consider tutoring or becoming involved in one-time projects that help kids.

Once you're ready to mentor a young person, you can contact one of the following agencies to learn how you can mentor a child in need right in your own community.

America's Promise 888-55-YOUTH
Big Brothers Big Sisters of America 215-567-7000
National Council of Volunteer Centers 800-59-LIGHT
100 Black Men of America 404-688-5100
National Mentoring Partnership 202-729-4340
Salvation Army 703-684-5500

We can inspire our nation's children to care about the future, to have compassion, and to have integrity by getting them involved in service right away. The only hope for a world that transcends selfishness is to create a litle bit of heaven on earth.

TEN MINI-MIRACLES
YOU CAN DO TO CHANGE YOUR WORLD

1. Buy a handful of ride tickets at a carnival that's visiting your town. (Ask the carnival manager to match your purchase.) Donate the tickets to a youth agency, like the Boys and Girls Club, so

economically disadvantaged kids can enjoy the fun.

2. If you're driving and see kids crossing a busy street without a crossing guard, get out of your car and help them safely cross the street.

3. Pay the p.t.a. membership dues for a low-income parent who has children in the school. You can make an anonymous payment by doubling your annual fee and by including a note that reads, "Please use the extra membership dues to sign up a parent who otherwise would not be able to afford to join."

4. While it may be tempting to sell a used computer, you will almost always come out on top if you donate it to an educational institution. When you donate a computer to a nonprofit organization, the fair market value can be claimed as a charitable contribution. Contact Gifts in Kind International, 333 North Fairfax Street, Alexandria, Virginia 22314; (703) 836-2121, to donate a used computer.

5. If you know a child who does not have medical insurance, encourage the child's parent or legal guardian to enroll him or her in the Children's Health Matters (CHM) program. CHM helps

enroll uninsured children in Medicaid to ensure their access to quality health care. Visit www. childrenshealthmatters.org for more information.

6. Remind your neighborhood convenience store not to sell cigarettes and alcohol to minors. If they do, report it to authorities immediately.

7. At the office, take up a collection of bus tokens and subway passes and donate them to a public school, where they can be given to poor students who cannot afford transportation to and from school. Be sure to contact the school prior to the collection to make sure they can use the tokens and passes.

8. Empty your medicine cabinet of unused medicines still in their original packaging that have at least one year left before the expiration date (e.g., aspirin, acetaminophen, vitamins, antibiotics). Send these medications to the World Concern Supply Service. They will be donated to the poorest nations, such as Haiti and Mongolia. Contact World Concern Supply Service, 19303 Fremont Avenue North, Seattle, Washington 98133; (800) 755-5022.

9. During the first week of school, many young children who arrive by bus need help finding

their classrooms in the morning. Volunteer every morning the first week of school to help tots find their way around. From the time they hop off the bus to the moment they pledge allegiance to the flag (usually between 7:45 and 8:00 A.M.), you can ensure that tiny tykes find their way safe and sound.

10. Donate used ski equipment to the Special Olympics. Call (800) 700-8585 for more information, or you can donate at a participating sporting goods store.

COPYCAT KINDNESS

All mankind is divided into three classes:
those that are immovable, those that are movable,
and those that move.

— MUSLIM PROVERB

You picked up this book to learn how to make a difference in the world. Now, when you read the newspaper or watch the television news, you won't be idle with despair: You have the skills and knowledge to help others.

But there's strength in numbers. The more who help, the more our world changes for the better. So getting others to pitch in can actually be a mini-miracle in itself. How can you get others to help? Use copycat kindness.

When I was sixteen years old, I was disturbed by a student's comments in health class about people living with AIDS. She said that people who contracted the virus deserved it: They had done an "evil thing" and this was the "consequence of their actions." What dismayed me even more was that this was the general consensus among other students in the class. In a conservative community like Berks County, Pennsylvania, where the number of new AIDS cases each year is among Pennsylvania's highest, this view is not uncommon. Didn't anyone else believe that we must be kind and compassionate to all people? I decided to work not only to help students feel compassionate about people with AIDS while they learned the truth about the disease but also to assist a local AIDS hospice.

As a teenager myself, I knew that preaching compassion to kids would be the wrong approach. Instead, I believed that if students had the opportunity to actually interact with HIV-positive people — by cooking meals, striking up conversations, playing games, and just developing friendships with them — then their innate compassion would shine through. Eventually, these interactions would bring them to reassess the many misconceptions about AIDS they had been exposed to.

Whenever I'd started a new project in the past, I never had a problem finding eager volunteers. Even when the task was unappealing, like hauling smelly tires from a mosquito-infested swamp during the hot summer months, I always had more help than I needed. So I was surprised to find that after a week of desperately trying to recruit kids to join me for a Saturday evening volunteer project at an AIDS hospice, a friend and I were the only ones to sign up.

I couldn't blame these kids for not wanting to get involved: Despite the curriculum taught in most American high schools, which broke down stereotypes and taught preventive measures to curtail the spread of AIDS, students at my school were still left in the dark. Many were ignorant: One student said she wouldn't travel to major cities in the summer because she feared a mosquito that bit an HIV-positive person might bite her next and thus she would contract the virus. I saw that I really had no reason to be angry with my classmates for not volunteering; they simply didn't know the facts. Instead of giving up, I used copycat kindness to get them involved.

Copycat kindness involves setting an example for others. I reasoned that if my classmates saw how much satisfaction and fun I received from consistently volunteering every weekend at the hospice, they'd want to volunteer, too.

So every Saturday, my friend and I cooked sumptuous vegetarian meals for the staff and residents of the hospice. We set the tables, struck up conversations, and even helped decorate the hospice to reflect a holiday theme. After every meal, we took the time to wash all the dishes, tidy the industrial-size kitchen, and carefully wrap leftover food for residents to enjoy later that evening.

At school, I only spoke about the project if someone asked first. That was important. To avoid sounding preachy, I would only talk honestly and not necessarily always glowingly about my volunteer experience. This way, my classmates could intelligently weigh whether or not they'd want to volunteer at the hospice.

In just a few months, young people in my school were able to face their fears of people living with AIDS. Through copycat kindness, an example was set that they soon wanted to follow. Eventually, the program became so popular with students at my school that my own volunteer services were no longer needed at the hospice.

Rekindling Kindness in Others

Pleading, begging, or "guilting" someone into helping others will never, ever work. But you can always try to help rekindle someone's Angel Power by using copycat kindness. The key is to find your own joy in service.

My parents and my older brother, David, immigrated from South Korea to the United States in 1973 with a few hundred dollars and two suitcases. My father had big dreams for his family and knew the United States could help bring him wealth, opportunity, and happiness.

As a young man who studied medicine in South Korea, my father began his career as a training physician in Buffalo, New York. Eventually, he settled in Reading, Pennsylvania, to start a practice; he quickly became a popular doctor at the hospital and was notorious for his unusual practice of singing at the top of his lungs to patients before surgery in an attempt to soothe their nerves. My father's singing embarrassed me as a child, but later on, I realized it was an interesting quirk that actually helped others at a vulnerable time.

Soon, my father was earning enough to be considered wealthy by American standards. But he never forgot his roots and he saved, invested wisely, and knew the value of a dollar; for years, he never drove a fancy car, as his peers did. His financial savvy paid for my brother's and sister's college education (I still have a college fund waiting to be spent, "just in case") and bought two homes on the East Coast. Our family always embarked on fun vacations and had plenty of food to eat and clothing to wear.

My father's financial caution, though, was contradictory to my desire to give generously to those in need. As a child, I donated birthday and holiday money to charity. This drove my parents insane. So much so that when they gave me money for groceries (we bought groceries separately so their meat products wouldn't touch my veggie food), I had to promise that I wouldn't give the money away. My father wished I would save instead of giving so much to others.

My parents grew up with nothing, came to the United States with almost nothing, and worked tirelessly to create a successful life for themselves. I do not deny that I had a privileged upbringing and probably can't fathom the struggle my parents had to endure when they were young. (It wasn't until I moved to Washington, D.C., that I learned that cable television wasn't free.) The reason I wanted to give to charity was that I appreciated the opportunities given to me. As Suze Orman, author of *The 9 Steps to Financial Freedom,* said, "The impulse to give...puts you in touch with the best part of yourself—and the principles of abundance that are alive in the world."

I had the freedom to pursue my beliefs and goals, and my parents could see how fulfilling and satisfying even the simplest acts of generosity could be. One day—boom—their feelings changed. As if a lightbulb had been switched on, my parents suddenly began to support a number of worthy causes. They saw that being generous could also put them in touch with the best part of being human.

This was such a meaningful moment for me. My parents had taught me so much about life, had provided so much to me, had supported me unconditionally. Finally, I was able to share a lesson with them, too.

TEN MINI-MIRACLES
YOU CAN DO TO CHANGE YOUR WORLD

1. One out of nine women in the United States will develop breast cancer in her lifetime. Schedule a screening mammogram for your mother, daughter, friend, or grandmother. According to the National Alliance of Breast Cancer Organizations, breast cancer can be treated effectively if detected early enough, with a five-year survival rate of more than ninety-seven percent.

2. Donate a used tennis racket to the Rackets-for-Kids program of the Tennis Industry Association. To date, more than 43,000 rackets have been given to young people who would otherwise be unable to participate in the game of tennis. Write the Tennis Industry Association at 200 Castlewood Drive, North Palm Beach, Florida, 33408.

3. Notify your loved ones and sign up to become an organ donor. In most states, you can sign up when you renew your driver's license at the department of motor vehicles.

4. Donate used compact discs to the local public library; the CD's will be put into circulation so patrons can borrow different types of music. Or you can sell your compact discs to a used-music store and donate the proceeds to your favorite charity.

5. Participate in Nike's Rescue-a-Shoe program. Through the program, Nike recycles used athletic shoes and grinds them into small pieces. This "retired" footwear is then given new life as surfacing for playgrounds, tennis courts, basketball courts, and running tracks. Since 1994, more than one hundred sports surfaces have been created across the country. Call (800) 929-PLAY for more information.

6. When you join an organization like the National Wildlife Federation, Amnesty International, or the Humane Society of the United States, you often receive a monthly or quarterly magazine with your membership. Donate your free subscription to a school or public library.

7. Participate in the annual Kick Butts Day sponsored by the Campaign for Tobacco-Free Kids. Help kids fight back against the tobacco industry's marketing efforts by sending a powerful

message that kids are a force to be reckoned with. When you call (800) 284-KIDS, you can send a free fax to your representative in Congress supporting current legislation to battle the powerful tobacco industry. Visit www.kickbuttsday.org for more information.

8. Donate used ice skates to help inner-city youth. Write to Friends of the Kelly Rink at P.O. Box 629, Jamaica Plain, Massachusetts, 02130 to help.

9. Donate food to a food collection agency during the summer months (rather than during the holiday season), when kids aren't in school and therefore create a greater burden on the family's financial resources.

10. Send used—even defective—hearing aids to Hear Now, a nonprofit organization that repairs hearing aids and provides them to low-income people in the United States with hearing impairments. Contact Hear Now at (800) 648-4327.

Angel Power Rule #10

WHEN ONE PLUS ONE EQUALS THREE

Make no mistake about it: I'm doing this for myself.

—ANITA RODDICK,
FOUNDER OF THE BODY SHOP

I've said it before: When you extend yourself to someone in need or help improve your community, your own life will begin to change. But how does donating an old bicycle to charity make you a better person?

I believe the missing link between achieving success and experiencing the joy of personal fulfillment is the selfless act of making a difference in the world. To be selfless is actually to be selfish; your selfless acts will encourage feelings of happiness to flourish beyond your wildest dreams.

"When one plus one equals three" isn't the easiest concept to explain in words. When you combine your daily career and family life with the skills, achievements, and personal fulfillment from your mini-miracle work, everything is affected positively. For example, when you do something to help those in need, your compassion may extend itself to the workplace, helping you develop more productive relationships with fellow employees. You become a better person, your spirit improves, and you project a positive vibe to those around you.

Losing a sense of self-worth can be very scary — that I know from experience. It affects all aspects of your life: your career, your relationship with your significant other, friends, and family. But it can also be a positive experience that may lead you back onto the right path in life.

When I was eighteen years old, I stepped down as CEO of Earth 2000 National; it was a bittersweet moment for me. On the one hand, I suddenly had lots of free time to take up a hobby, work out at the gym, and just sit back and relax. On the other hand, after one day of doing nothing, I was bored out of my mind.

But what I thought was boredom I later discovered was depression. At the time, I thought maybe all I needed was a change of scenery. So I moved out of my parents' home in Reading, Pennsylvania, to

Washington, D.C., to work as a public relations consultant. The experience of living in a big city with plenty of cultural opportunities, a chance to lobby my elected officials any day I pleased, and terrific vegetarian restaurants were all great reasons to move there.

But a month after moving into my first apartment I found myself in a real funk. I was sipping coffee one morning and thought to myself, I hate my life.

I was taken aback. Why would I think such a horrible thing?

I couldn't pinpoint it at that moment, but I later realized I hadn't done any volunteering in months. When I was working at Earth 2000, I woke up very early in the morning and looked forward to campaigning, volunteering, and interacting with staff and members. Now that I wasn't part of a charity, I was depressed, unmotivated, and—I hate to admit it—apathetic.

Once I figured out the cause of my depression, I did two things. First, I wrote a check to a charitable organization in the amount of two hundred dollars. That was an awful lot of money to me then, but I knew I could afford it if I clipped coupons and didn't buy that sweater I had had my eye on for some time. Second, I grabbed a trash bag and bought a pair of work gloves for $1.99. Because I had to go to work that day, I was dressed up in a nice suit and tie, but was determined to follow through with my mini-miracle project anyway. For a whole hour, I cleaned up a park near my home, all by myself, during my lunch break. Dozens of other workers in their own nice suits saw me and probably thought I had lost my mind, but I didn't care. I felt good.

That day, my spirit was high, I got myself out of my funk, and I felt good about myself. When I feel good, I can make good business decisions for myself, be kind and generous to my friends, be tolerant of people who would normally frustrate me, and keep my life in order. Being selfless by creating mini-miracles, I discovered, was a genuine way to lift my spirits.

A Well-Rounded Life

Despite all the self-help gurus who promise "personal power" if you order their expensive cassette tapes or attend one of their three-day seminars at the airport Marriott, the most powerful and enduring things you can do to improve your spirit are to lead with your heart, be realistic, and try to do good in the world.

Trust me. I've hugged trees in redwood forests trying to "find myself." I've pretended to be an animal, worn a paper mask shaped like a bumblebee, and talked in the "spirit of the bee" about what makes me happy, what makes me sad, and what humans do to hurt their fellow "bees." I've also been a participant in way too many sharing circles. Here's the point: There was a moment in my life when I realized this was not a form of self-improvement that would ever work for me.

That's why this book is a mix of practicality and inspiration. Most of us will probably not achieve fulfillment from walking across hot coals or running barefoot through a forest declaring our love for Mother Earth and her creations. Fulfillment comes from allowing ourselves to be inspired, to think and act from a practical point of view, and to create mini-miracles for someone in need or for our community.

That's the path I have chosen. It has strengthened my spirit and affected my career, my relations with friends and family, and my overall emotional well-being for the better. When you allow altruism to become part of your life, something almost magical happens; the feeling is difficult to describe, but you'll know it when it happens. The sensation is real and everlasting. It's called true happiness.

RESOURCE GUIDE

Addresses, telephone numbers, and URL addresses are subject to change. For an updated list, please visit my Web site, www.dannyseo.com.

100 Black Men of America
141 Auburn Avenue
Atlanta, GA 30303
(404) 688-5100

America's Promise
909 North Washington
   Street
Suite 400
Alexandria, VA 22314
(888) 55-YOUTH
www.americaspromise.org

American Cancer Society
1875 Connecticut Avenue,
   NW
Suite 730
Washington, DC 20009
(800) ACS-2345
www.cancer.org.

Bargemusic
Fulton Ferry Landing
Brooklyn, NY 11201
(718) 624-4061

Big Brothers Big Sisters of
America
230 North 13 Street
Philadelphia, PA 19107-1538
(215) 567-7000
www.bbbsa.org

Community Cousins
200 Saxony Road
Encinitas, CA 92024
(760) 944-2899

Michael Crisler
3411 East Colorado Avenue
Denver, CO 80210

The Eden Alternative
742 Turnpike Road
Sherburne, NY 13460
(607) 674-5232
www.edenalt.com

The Fatherhood Project
330 Seventh Avenue
14th Floor
New York, NY 10001
(212) 465-2044
www.familiesandwork.org

The Garden Project
Pier 28
San Francisco, CA 94105

Habitat for Humanity
International
121 Habitat Street
Americus, GA 31709-3498
(800) HABITAT
www.habitat.org

Happy Helpers for the
Homeless
403A Old Stage Road
Glen Burnie, MD 21061

Help for the Harvest
9603 108 Avenue North
Largo, FL 33773

Kids Konnected
P.O. Box 603
Trabuco Canyon, CA 92678
(949) 380-4334
www.kidskonnected.org

Listening Post
3100 Cherry Creek South
    Drive
Suite 1404
Denver, CO 80209-3226

Ms. Foundation for Women
120 Wall Street
33rd Floor
New York, NY 10005
(212) 742-2300
www.ms.foundation.org

Points of Light Foundation
1400 I Street, NW
Suite 800
Washington, DC 20005
(800) 59-LIGHT
www.pointsoflight.org

National Mentoring
    Partnership
1400 I Street, NW
Suite 850
Washington, DC 20005
(202) 729-4345
www.mentoring.org

Operation Clean Slate
1578 Minorca Drive
Costa Mesa, CA 92626

Parents of Watts
10828 Lou Dillon
Los Angeles, CA 90059

Redistribution Center
7736 Hoyt Circle
Arvada, CO 80005

Salvation Army
P.O. Box 269
Alexandria, VA 22313
(703) 684-5500
www.salvationarmy.org

Stand for Children
1834 Connecticut Avenue,
    NW
Washington, DC 20009
(202) 234-0095
www.stand.org

TreePeople
12601 Mulholland Drive
Beverly Hills, CA 90210
(818) 753-4600
www.treepeople.org